THE
INDIAN
Grammar

BEGUN

D1596332

THE INDIAN Grammar

BEGUN: OR,

An Essay to bring the Indian Language

INTO

RULES,

For the Help of such as desire to Learn the same, for the furtherance of the Gospel among them.

BY *JOHN ELIOT*

With Foreword by
Caring Hands
SACHEM OF THE NATICK PRAYING INDIANS

APPLEWOOD BOOKS
BEDFORD, MASSACHUSETTS

This edition of *The Indian Grammar Begun* has been brought back to life after 335 years by Roger "Looks Twice" Gordy, a book designer. Four years ago Roger and his best friend Sheila "She Who Finds Things" Williams met Caring Hands and her family, descendants of the Natick Praying Indians, who were one of the three drums and singers at a powwow in South Natick, Massachusetts. Over a two year period of time Roger and Sheila became very close friends with Caring Hands and learned of her interest in learning the Massachusett language of her people. Sheila found a microfilm copy of John Eliot's Indian Bible and printed out all 650 pages which was then gifted to Caring Hands and her family at a powwow at Cochituate State Park. Two years later Roger came across a listing that there was a microfilm copy of John Eliot's *The Indian Grammar* originally printed in 1666. Rather than just printing out the microfilm, Roger decided that he could scan the microfilm printout and then by hand clean up the original type in Adobe Photoshop, pixel by pixel. He also chose to retype the document letter for letter in modern Caslon (the original was set in Caslon as lead type) and eliminate the long "s" that is often mistaken for an "f". By placing the cleaned up original next to the modern type any question as to the correct spelling of the Massachusett words would be eliminated. If there is a type mistake it would be in the original as well. It is Roger's hope that by bringing *The Indian Grammar* back in-print with the help of Applewood Books, that a language long lost will again be spoken and eventually written.

March 2001

ISBN I-55709-575-2

Thank you for purchasing an Applewood Book. Applewood reprints America's lively classics—books from the past that are of interest to modern readers. For a free copy of our current catalog, write to Applewood Books, P.O. Box 365, Bedford, MA 01730.

Library of Congress Control Number: 2005932171

Dedicated to

Caring Hands
and
She Who Finds Things

FOREWORD

In 1631, the Reverend John Eliot sailed from England to the "New" England of the Americas. In 1651 his missionary efforts culminated in the establishment of the first Praying Indian Village of Natick.

Eliot, also known as the "Apostle to the Indians," is best known for publishing the first Bible on American soil. The translation into the Natick–Massachusett Indian language, an exclusively oral language, remains one of the most phenomenal linguistic contributions in history.

Many colonists were interested in understanding the native language, which prompted Eliot to pen a grammatical representation. Eliot had no written reference for this complex language other than his own Bible translation and aptly entitled this new work *Indian Grammar Begun*. Although the original text was written for English speaking non-natives, today many Algonkian Natives utilize Eliot's works for their language reaffirmation and/or spirituality.

The manner in which Roger Gordy presents a "side by side" comparison with the original text is superb. The format allows the reader to appreciate the complexity of the language, and retain its 17TH century character. The text's readability and level of phonetic clarity qualifies it as a substantial educational tool.

As tribal leader and teacher of the young, I wish to express appreciation to Mr. Gordy for assuming this task and Applewood Books for making the text available to us. Kuttabotomish to the Reverend John Eliot, whose gifts to our people have spanned over 350 years and continue to reach his beloved Praying Indians.

To all my relations, all His creations and harmony to the Great Tribe . . . the tribe of the human race I say Ahho.

Caring Hands, Touohkomuck Silva Clan
Sachem Natick Praying Indians.
March 2001

THE
INDIAN
Grammar
BEGUN: *OR,*
An Essay to bring the Indian Language
INTO
RULES,

For the Help of such as desire to Learn the same, for
the furtherance of the Gospel among them.

BY *JOHN ELIOT.*

Isa.33.19. *Thou shalt not see a fierce people, a people of a deeper speech then
thou canst perceive, of a stammering tongue, that thou canst not understand.*
Isa.66.18. *It shall come that I will gather all Nations and Tongues, and they
shall come and see my Glory.*
Dan.7.14. *And there was given him Dominion, and Glory, and a Kingdome,
that all People, Nations and Languages should serve him, &c.*
Psal.19.3. *There is no speech nor language where their voice is not heard.*
Mal.3.11. *From the rising of the Sun, even to the going down of the same, my
Name shall be great among the Gentiles, &c.*

CAMBRIDGE:
Printed by *Marmaduke Johnson.* 1 6 6 6.

THE
INDIAN
Grammar

BEGUN: OR,

An Essay to bring the Indian Language

INTO
RULES,

For the Help of such as desire to Learn the same, for the furtherance of the Gospel among them.

BY *JOHN ELIOT*

CAMBRIDGE:

Printed by *Marmaduke Johnson.*   1666.

To the Right Honourable,

ROBERT BOYLE Esq;

GOVERNOUR:

With the rest of the Right Honourable and Christian

CORPORATION

For the Propagation of the *GOSPEL* unto
the *INDIANS* in *New England.*

NOBLE SIR,

YOu were pleased, among other Testimonies of your Christian and prudent care for the effectual Progress
of this great Work of the Lord Jesus among
the Inhabitants of these Ends of the Earth,
and goings down of the Sun, to Command
me (for such an aspect have your so wise and
seasonable Motions, to my heart) to Compile
a Grammar of this Language, for the help
of others who have an heart to study and learn

A 2   the

To the Right Honorable,

ROBERT BOYLE Esq;

G O V E R N O U R :

With the rest of the Right Honorable and Christian

CORPORATION

For the Propagation of the *GOSPEL* unto
the I N D I A N S in *New England.*

NOBLE SIR,

You *were pleased, among other Testimonies of your Christian and prudent care for the effectual Progress of this great Work of the Lord Jesus among the Inhabitants of these Ends of the Earth, and goings down of the Sun, to* Command me *(for such an aspect have your so wise and seasonable Motions, to my heart) to Compile a* Grammar *of this Language, for the help of others who have an heart to study and learn*

A 2

the same, for the sake of Christ, and of the poor Souls of these Ruines of Mankinde, among whom the Lord is now about a Resurrection-work, to call them into his holy Kingdome. I have made an Essay unto this difficult Service, and laid together some Bones and Ribs preparatory at least for such a work. It is not worthy the Name of a Grammar, but such as it is, I humbly present it to your Honours, and request your Animadversions upon the Work, and Prayers unto the Lord for blessing upon all Essayes and Endeavours for the promoting of his Glory, and the Salvation of the Souls of these poor People. Thus humbly commending your Honours unto the blessing of Heaven and to the guidance of the Word of God, which is able to save your Souls, I remain

Your Honours Servant in the Service
of our Lord Jesus,

JOHN ELIOT.

the same, for the sake of Christ, and of the poor Souls of these Ruines of Mankinde, among whom the Lord is now about a Resurrection-work, to call them into his holy Kingdom. I have made an Essay unto this difficult Service, and laid together some Bones and Ribs preparatory at least for such a work. It is not worthy the Name of a Grammar, but such as it is, I humbly present it to your Honours, and request your Animadversions upon the Work, and Prayers unto the Lord for blessing upon all Essayes and Endeavours for the promoting of his Glory, and the Salvation of the Souls of these poor People. Thus humbly commending your Honours unto the blessing of Heaven and to the guidance of the Word of God, which is able to save your Souls, I remain

Your Honours Servant in the Service of our Lord Jesus,

JOHN ELIOT.

THE
INDIAN GRAMMAR
B E G V N.

GRAMMAR is the *Art* or *Rule of speaking.*

There be two parts of *Grammar* :
1. The *Art of making* words.
2. The *Art of ordering* words for speech.

The Art of *making* words, is
1. By various *articulate sounds.*
2. By *regular composing* of them.

Articulate sounds are composed into
Syllables.
Words.

The various *articulate sounds* must be distinguished
By
Names.
Characters.

These *Names* and *Characters* do make the *Alpha-bet.*

Because the *English Language* is the first, and most attainable Language which the *Indians* learn, he is a learned man among them, who can *Speak*, *Reade* and *write* the *English Tongue.*

I therefore use the same *Characters* which are of most common use in our English Books ; *viz.* the *Roman* and *Italick* Letters.

Also our *Alpha-bet* is the same with the *English*, saving in these few things following.

1. The *difficulty of the Rule* about the Letter [*c*], by reason of the *change of its sound* in the five sounds, *ca ce ci co cu* ; being sufficiently helped by the Letters [*k* and *s.*] : We therefore lay

A 3

THE
INDIAN GRAMMAR
BEGUN.

GRAMMAR is the *Art* or *Rule of speaking.*
There be two parts of *Grammar* :
1. The *Art* of *making words.*
2. the *Art* of *ordering words* for speech.

The Art of *making words,* is
{
1. By various articulate *sounds.*
2. By *regular composing* of them.
}

Articulate sounds are composed into
{
Syllables.
Words.
}

The various *articulate sounds* must be distinguished
By
{
Names.
Characters.
}

These *Names* and *Characters* do make the *Alpha-bet.*

Because the *English Language* is the first, and most attainable Language which the *Indians* learn, he is a learned man among them, who can *Speak*, *Reade* and *Write* the *English Tongue.*

I therefore use the same *Characters* which are of most common use in our English Books; *viz.* the *Roman* and *Italick* Letters.

Also our *Alpha-bet* is the same with the *English,* saving in these few things following.

1. The *difficulty of the Rule* about the Letter [c], by reason of the *change of its sound* in the five sounds, *ca ce ci co cu* ; being sufficiently helped by the Letters [*k* and *s.*] : We therefore

A 3

lay by the Letter [*c*], faving in [*ch*] ; of which there is frequent ufe in the Language.   Yet I do not put it out of the *Alpha-bet*, for the ufe of it in other Languages, but the Character [*ch*] next to it, and call it [*chee*].

2. I put [*i*] Confonant into our *Alpha-bet*, and give it this Character [*j*], and call it *ji*, or [*gi*], as this Syllable foundeth in the Englifh word [*giant*] ; and I place it next after [*i vocal*]. And I have done thus, becaufe it is a *regular found* in the *third perfon fingular* in the *Imperative Mode* of Verbs, which cannot well be diftinguifhed without it : though I have fometimes ufed [*gh*] in ftead of it, but it is harder and more inconvenient.   The proper found of it is, as the Englifh word [*age*] foundeth.   See it ufed *Genef.*1. 3,6,9,11.

3. We give (*v*) Confonant a *diftinct name*, by putting together (*u f.*) or (*uph*), and we never ufe it , fave when it foundeth as it doth in the word (*fave, have*), and place it next after (*u* vocal.) Both thefe Letters (*u* Vocal, and *v* Confonant) are together in their proper founds in the Latine word (*uva*, a Vine.)

4. We call *w* (*wee*), becaufe our name giveth no hint of the *power* of its found.

Thefe Confonants (*l. n. r.*) have fuch a *natural coincidence*, that it is an eminent variation of their dialects.

We *Maffachufets* pronounce the *n*.   The *Nipmuk Indians* pronounce *l*.   And the *Northern Indians* pronounce *r*.   As inftance :

We fay   *Anúm*   (*um* produced ⎤
Nipmuk,   *Alúm*   ⎬ A Dog.
Northern, *Arúm*   ⎦   So in moft words.

Our *Vocals* are five :   *a e i o u.*   Dipthongs, or *double founds*, are many, and of much ufe.

ai au ei ee eu eau oi oo ∞.

Efpecially we have more frequent ufe of [o *and* ∞] then other Languages have : and our [∞] doth alwayes found as it doth in thefe Englifh words (*moody, book.*)

We

lay by the Letter [*c*], saving in [*ch*]; of which there is frequent use in the Language. Yet I do not put it out of the *Alpha-bet*, for the use of it in other Languages, but the Character [*ch*] next to it, and call it [*chee*].

2. I put [*i*] Consonant into our *Alpha-bet*, and give it this Character [*j*], and call it *ji*, or [*gi*], as this Syllable soundeth in the English word [*giant*], and I place it next after [*i* vocal]. And I have done thus, because it is a *regular sound* in the *third person singular* in the *Imperative Mode* of Verbs, which cannot well be distinguished without it: though I have sometimes used [*gh*] in stead of it, but it is harder and more inconvenient. The proper sound of it is, as the English word [*age*] soundeth. See it used *Gene*s. 1.3,6,9,11.

3. We give (*v*) Consonant a *distinct name*, by putting together (*úf.*) or (*uph*), and we never use it, save when it soundeth as it doth in the word (*save, have*), and place it next after (*u* vocal.) Both these Letters (*u* Vocal, and *v* Consonant) are together in their proper sounds in the Latine word (*uva*, a Vine.)

4. We call *w* (*wee*), because our name giveth no hint of the *power* of its sound.

These Consonants (*l. n. r.*) have such a *natural coincidence*, that it is an eminent variation of their dialects.

We *Massachusets* pronounce the *n*. The *Nipmuk Indians* pronounce *l*. And the *Northern Indians* pronounce *r*. As instance:

We say	*Anúm*	(*um* produced)	⎫
Nipmuk,	*Alúm*		⎬ A Dog.
Northern,	*Arúm*		⎭ So in most words.

Our *Vocals* are five: *a   e   i   o   u*. Dipthongs, or *double sounds*, are many, and of much use.

ai au ei ee eu eau oi oo ∞.

Especially we have more frequent use of [o *and* ∞] then other Languages have: and our [∞] doth always sound as it doth in these English words (*moody, book*.)

We ufe onely *two Accents,* and but *fometime.* The *Acute* (') to fhew which Syllable is firft *produced* in pronouncing of the word; which if it be not attended, no Nation can underftand their own Language: as appeareth by the *witty Conceit* of the *Tytere tu's.*

o̓ produced with the accent, is a *regular diftinction* betwixt the *firft* and *fecond perfons plural* of the *Suppofitive Mode* ; as

{ Naumog, *If* we *fee* : (as in *Log.*)
{ Naumóg, *If ye fee* : (as in *Vogue.*)

The other *Accent* is (^), which I call *Nafal* ; and it is ufed onely upon (*o̓*) when it is founded in the Nofe, as oft it is ; or upon (*a̓*) for the like caufe.

This is a *general Rule,* When two (o o) come together, ordinarily the *firft* is *produced* ; and fo when two (∞) are together.

All the *Articulate founds* and *Syllables* that ever I heard (with obfervation) in their Language, are fufficiently comprehended and ordered by our *Alpha-bet,* and the *Rules* here fet down.

Character.	Name.	Character.	Name.
a		n	en
b	bee	o	
c	fee	p	pee
ch	chee	q	keúh
d	dee	r	ar
e		ſ s	eſ
f	ef	t	tee
g	gee *as in* geefe	u	
h		v	vf
i		w	wee
j	ji *as in* giant	x	ex
k	ka	y	wy
l	el	z	zad.
m	em		

Here be 27 *Characters* : The reafon of *increafing the number* is above.

And I have been thus far bold with the *Alpha-bet,* becaufe it is the firft time of *writing this Language* ; and it is better to fettle our *Foundation* right at firft, then to have it to *mend afterwards.*

Mufical

3 *The* Indian *Grammar begun.*

We use only *two Accents*, and but *sometime.* The *Acute* (´) to shew which Syllable is first *produced* in pronouncing of the word; which if it be not attended, no Nation can understand their own Language: as appeareth, by the *witty Conceit* of the *Tytere tu's.*

ó produced with the accent, is a *regular distinction* betwixt the *first* and *second persons plural* of the *Suppositive Mode* ; as

{Naumog, *If we see* : (as in *Log.*)
{Naumóg, *If ye see* : (as in *Vogue.*)

The other *Accent* is (ˆ), which I call *Nasal* ; and it is used only upon (*ô*) when it is sounded in the Nose, as often it is; or upon *(â)* for the like cause.

This is a *general Rule,* When two (o o) come together, ordinarily the *first* is *produced* ; and so when two (∞) are together.

All the *Articulate sounds* and *Syllables* that ever I heard (with observation) in their Language, are sufficiently comprehended and ordered by our *Alpha-bet,* and the *Rules* here set down.

Character.	Name.	Character.	Name.
a		n	en
b	bee	o	
c	see	p	pee
ch	chee	q	keúh
d	dee	r	ar
e		s	es
f	ef	t	tee
g	gee *as in* geese	u	
h		v	vf
i		w	wee
j	ji *as in* giant	x	ex
k	ka	y	wy
l	el	z	zad.
m	em		

Here be 27 *Characters* : The reason of *increasing the number* is above.

And I have been thus far bold with the *Alpha-bet,* because it is the first time of *writing this Language* ; and it is better to settle our *Foundation* right at first, then to have it to *mend afterwards.*

Muſical ſounds they alſo have, and *perfeﬅ Harmony,* but they differ from us in *ſound.*

There be four ſeveral ſorts of *Sounds* or *Tones* uttered by Mankinde.

1. *Articulation* in Speech.
2. *Laughter.*
3. *Latation* and *Joy:* of which kinde of *ſounds* our *Muſick* and *Song* is made.
4. *Ululation, Howling, Yelling,* or *Mourning:* and of that kinde of *ſound* is their *Muſick* and *Song* made.

In which kinde of *ſound* they alſo *hallow* and *call,* when they are moſt vociferous.

And that it is thus, it may be perceived by this, that their Language is ſo full of (∞) and ô *Naſal.*

They have *Harmony* and *Tunes* which they ſing, but the matter. is not in *Metter.*

They are much pleaſed to have their Language and Words in *Metter* and *Rithme,* as it now is in *The ſinging Pſalms* in ſome poor meaſure, enough to *begin* and *break the ice* withall : Theſe they ſing in *our Muſicall Tone.*

So much *for the* Sounds *and* Characters.

Now follows the Conſideration of Syllables, *and the* Art *of* Spelling.

THe *formation of Syllables* in their Language, doth in nothing differ from the *formation of Syllables* in the *Engliſh,* and other *Languages.*

When I taught our *Indians* firſt to lay out a Word into *Syllables,* and then according to the *ſound* of every Syllable to make it up with the *right Letters,* viz. if it were a *ſimple ſound,* then *one Vocall* made the Syllable ; if it were ſuch a *ſound* as required ſome of the *Conſonants* to make it up, then the *adding* of the *right Conſonants* either *before* the Vocall, or *after* it, or *both.* They quickly apprehended and underſtood this *Epitomie* of the *Art of Spelling,* and could ſoon learn to *Reade.*

The

4 *The* Indian *Grammar begun.*

Musical sounds they also have, and *perfect Harmony,* but they differ from us in *sound.*

There be four several sorts of *Sounds* or *Tones* uttered by Mankinde.

1. *Articulation* in Speech.
2. *Laughter.*
3. *Lætation* and *Joy* : of which kinde of *sounds* our *Musick* and *Song* is made.
4. *Ululation, Howling, Yelling,* or *Mourning* : and of that kinde of *sound* is their *Musick* and *Song* made.

In which kinde of *sound* they also *hallow* and *call,* when they are most vociferous.

And that it is thus, it may be perceived by this, that their Language is so full of (∞) and ô *Nasal.*

They have *Harmony* and *Tunes* which they sing, but the matter is not in *Meeter.*

They are much pleased to have their Language and Words in *Meeter* and *Rithme,* as it now is in *The singing Psalms* in some poor measure, enough to *begin* and *break the ice* withall : These they sing in *our Musicall Tone.*

So much for the Sounds *and* Characters.

Now follows the Consideration of Syllables, *and the* Art *of* Spelling.

The *formation of Syllables* in their Language, doth in nothing differ from the *formation of Syllables* in the *English,* and other *Languages.*

When I taught our *Indians* first to lay out a Word into *Syllables,* and then according to the *sound* of every Syllable to make it up with the *right Letters,* viz. if it were a *simple sound,* then *one Vocall* made the Syllable; if it were such a *sound* as required some of the *Consonants* to make it up, then the *adding* of the *right Consonants* either *before* the Vocall, or *after* it, or *both.* They quickly apprehended and understood this *Epitomie* of the *Art of Spelling,* and could soon learn to *Reade.*

The *Men,* *Women,* and *up-grown* *Youth* do thus rationally learn to Reade: but the *Children* learn by *rote* and *cuftome,* as other Children do.

Such as defire to learn this Language, muft be attentive to *pronounce right,* efpecially to produce *that Syllable* that is *firft to be produced*; then they muft *Spell* by Art, and accuftome their *tongues* to pronounce their *Syllables* and *words*; then learn to reade fuch *Books* as are Printed in their Language. *Legendo, Scribendo, Loquendo,* are the *three means* to learn a Language.

So much for the Rule *of* Making Words.

Now follows the Ordering *of them for* Speech.

THe feveral forts of words are called *Parts of Speech,* which are in number *Seven.*

1. The *Pronoun.*
2. The *Noun.*   3. The *Adnoun,* or *Adjective.*
4. The *Verb.*   5. The *Adverb.*
6. The *Conjunction.*
7. The *Interjection.*

Touching thefe feveral kindes of Words, we are to confider,

1. The *formation* of them *afunder* by themfelves.
2. The *conftruction* of them, or the laying them together, to make *Senfe,* or *a Sentence.*

And thus far *Grammar* goeth in concatenation with *Logick:* for there is a *Reafon* of Grammar. The *laying of Sentences* together to make up a *Speech,* is performed by *Logick:* The *adorning* of that Speech with *Eloquence,* is performed by *Rhetorick.* Such a *ufe* and *accord* there is in thefe *generall Arts.*

In the *formation* of words *afunder* by themfelves,

Confider {
1. The *general Qualifications,* or *Affections* of words.
2. The *Kindes* of words.

B   The

5 *The* Indian *Grammar begun.*

The *Men, Women,* and *up-grown Youth* do thus rationally learn to Reade : but the *Children* learn by *rote* and *custome,* as other Children do.

Such as desire to learn this Language, must be attentive to *pronounce right,* especially to produce *that Syllable* that is *first to be produced* ; then they must *Spell* by Art, and accustome their *tongues* to pronounce their *Syllables* and *Words* ; then learn to reade such *Books* as are Printed in their Language. *Legendo, Scribendo, Lequendo,* are the *three means* to learn a Language.

So much for the Rule of Making Words.

Now follows the Ordering of them for Speech.

The several sorts of words are called *Parts of Speech,* which are in number *Seven.*

1. The *Pronoun.*
2. The *Noun.*   3. The *Adnoun,* or *Adjective.*
4. The *Verb.*   5. The *Adverb.*
6. The *Conjunction.*
7. The *Interjection.*

Touching these several kindes of Words, we are to consider,
1. The *formation* of them *asunder* by themselves.
2. The *construction* of them, or the laying them together, to make *Sense,* or *a Sentence.*

And thus far *Grammar* goeth in concatenation with *Logick* : for there is a *Reason* of *Grammar.* The *laying of Sentences* together to make up a *Speech,* is performed by *Logick* : The *adorning* of that Speech with *Eloquence,* is performed by *Rhetorick.* Such a *use* and *accord* there is in these *generall Arts.*

In the *formation* of words *asunder* by themselves,

Consider {
1. The *general Qualifications,* or *Affections* of words.
2. The *Kindes* of words.

B

The *Qualifications* are
{
1. In refpeſt of their *Rife* whence they fpring.
2. In refpeſt of their *Conforts* , how they are yoked.
}

In refpeſt of their *Rife,* fome are
{
1. *Original words : fua originis.*
2. *Ort words* fprung out of other :
Chiefly
{
Nominals : or *Verbs* made out of *Nouns.*
Verbals : or *Nouns* made out of *Verbs*
}
}

In refpeſt of *Conforts,* fome are
{
Simple words : one alone.
Compounded words : when two or more are made into one.
}

This Language doth greatly delight in *Compounding of words,* for Abbreviation, to *fpeak much* in *few words* , though they be fometimes *long* ; which is chiefly caufed by the *many Syllables* which the *Grammar Rule* requires, and *fuppletive Syllables* which are of no fignification , and curious care of *Euphonie.*

So much for the common Affeſtion of words.

Now follow the feverall Kindes of words.

THere be two kindes :
{
1. *Chief leading* words ;
{
Nouns.
Verbs.
}
2. Such as *attend upon,* and belong unto. the *chief leading words.*
}

Attendants on the *Chief,* are
{
1. Such as are *proper to each* ; as
{
Adnouns.
Adverbs.
}
2. Such as are of *common ufe to both* ; as
{
Pronouns.
Conjunſtions
}
}

Inde-

The *Qualifications* are { 1. In respect of their *Rise* whence they spring.

2. In respect of their *Consorts,* how they are yoked.

In respect of their *Rise,* some are {

1. *Original words: suæ originis.*
2. *Ort words* sprung out of other:

Chiefly { *Nominals:* or *Verbs* made out of *Nouns*
Verbals: or *Nouns* made out of *Verbs*

In respect of *Consorts,* some are { *Simple words:* one alone.
Compounded words: when two or more are made into one.

This Language doth greatly delight in *Compounding of words,* for Abbreviation, to *speak much* in *few words,* though they be sometimes *long;* which is chiefly caused by the *many Syllables* which the *Grammar Rule* requires, and *suppletive Syllables* which are of no signification , and curious care of *Euphonie.*

So much for the common Affection of words.

Now follow the severall Kindes *of words.*

There be two kindes: {

1. *Chief leading* words; { *Nouns.*
Verbs.

2. Such as *attend upon,* and belong unto the *chief leading words.*

Attendants on the *Chief,* are {

1. Such as are *proper to each; as* { *Adnouns.*
Adverbs.

2. Such as are of *common use to both* ; as { *Pronouns.*

Conjunctions.

Independent Paſſions or *Interjections* come under no *Series* or *Order*, but are of uſe in Speech, to expreſs the *paſſionate minde* of man.

Touching the *principal parts of Speech,* this may be ſaid in ge neral, That *Nouns* are the *names of Things,* and *Verbs* are the *names of Actions*; and therefore their *proper Attendants* are an ſwerable. *Adnouns* are the *qualities of Things,* and *Adverbs* are the *qualities of Actions.*

And hence is that wiſe Saying, *That a Chriſtian muſt be adorned with as many Adverbs as Adjectives:* He muſt as well *do good,* as *be good.* When a man's virtuous Actions are well adorned with *Ad verbs,* every one will conclude that the man is well adorned with virtuous *Adjectives.*

1. *Of the* Pronoun.

BEcauſe of the common and general uſe of the *Pronoun* to be affixed unto both *Nouns, Verbs,* and other *parts of Speech,* and that in the *formation* of them; therefore that is the *firſt Part of Speech* to be handled.

I ſhall give no other deſcription of them but this, They are ſuch words as do expreſs all the *perſons,* both *ſingular* and *plural:* as

Singular { Neen *I.* Ken *Thou.* Noh *or* nagum *He.* } *Plural* { Neenawun *or* kenawun,*We.* Kenaau *Ye.* Nahoh *or* nagoh, *They.* }

There be alſo other *Pronouns* of frequent uſe:

As the *Interrogative* of *perſons*; *ſing.* Howan. *pl.* Howanig,*Who*

The *Interrogative* of *things*; { *ſing.* Uttiyeu, or tanyeu. *pl.* Uttiyeuſh, *which.* }

Demonſtratives { of *perſons:* { *ſing.* Yeuoh,*This or that man.*Noh. *pl.* Yeug, *Theſe men.* Nag *or* neg, *They.* } of *things:* { Yeu *This.* Ne *This.* Yeuſh *Theſe.* Niſh *Theſe.* } }

B 2 *Diſtri-*

Independent Passions or *Interjections* come under no *Series* or *Order*, but are of use in Speech, to express the *passionate minde* of man.

Touching the *principal parts of Speech*, this may be said in general, That *Nouns* are *the names of Things*, and *Verbs* are the *names of Actions* ; and therefore their *proper Attendants* are answerable. *Adnouns* are *qualities of Things*, and *Adverbs* are the *qualities of Actions.*

And hence is that wise Saying, *That a Christian must be adorned with as many Adverbs as Adjectives* : He must as well *do good,* as *be good.* When a man's virtuous Actions are well adorned with *Adverbs,* every one will conclude that the man is well adorned with virtuous *Adjectives.*

1. *Of the Pronoun.*

Because of the common and general use of the *Pronoun* to be affixed unto both *Nouns, Verbs,* and other *parts of Speech,* and that in the *formation* of them; therefore that is the *first Part of Speech* to be handled.

I shall give no other description of them but this, They are such words as do express all the *persons,* both *singular* and *plural* : as

Singular { Neen *I.*
Ken *Thou.*
Noh *or* nagum *He.*

Plural { Neenawun *or* kenawun, *We.*
Kenaau *Ye.*
Nahoh *or* nagoh, *They.*

There be also other *Pronouns* of frequent use:
As the *Interrogative* of *persons* ; sing. Howan. *pl.* Howanig, *Who.*

The *Interrogative* of *things* ; { sing. Uttiyeu, *or* tanyeu.
pl. Uttiyeush, *Which.*

Demonstratives {
of *persons :* { sing. Yeuoh, *This or that man.* Noh.
pl. Yeug, *These men.* Nag *or* neg, *They.*

of *things :* { Yeu *This.* Ne *This.*
Yeush *These.* Nish *These.*

Diſtributives; as {Nawhutche, *ſome.* {Tohſuog ? {*How many?*
{Monaog, *many.*   {Tohſunaſh {

But becauſe theſe are not of uſe in *affixing* to other *Parts of Speech,* they may as well be reckoned among *Adnouns,* as ſome do; though there is another *Scheſis* upon them, and they attend upon *Verbs* as well as *Nouns.*

The *firſt* and *ſecond perſons* are of moſt uſe in affixing both of *Nouns* and *Verbs,* and other Parts of Speech.

The *third perſon ſingular* is affixed with ſuch Syllables *as theſe,* Wut. wun. um. ∞. *&c.* having reſpect to *Euphonie:* And ſometime the *third perſon,* eſpecially of *Verbs,* hath no *affix.*

Theſe *Pronouns,* (Neen *and* Ken) when they are affixed, they are *contracted into* Ne *and* Ke, and varied in the *Vocal* or *Vowel* according to *Euphonie,* with the word it is affixed unto; *as* N∞, K∞, *&c.*

If the word unto which it is affixed begin with a *Vocal,* then a *Conſonant* of a fitting ſound is interpoſed, to couple the word and his *affix* with an Euphonie: *as* Nut. kut. num. kum, *&c.*

I give not *Examples* of theſe *Rules,* becauſe they will be ſo obvious anon, when you ſee Nouns and Verbs *affixed.*

2. *Of a Noun.*

A *Noun* is a *Part of Speech* which ſignifieth *a thing*; or it is the *name of a thing.*

The *variation* of Nouns is not by *Male* and *Female,* as in other Learned Languages, and in *European Nations* they do.

Nor are they *varied* by *Caſes, Cadencies,* and *Endings:* herein they are more like to the *Hebrew.*

Yet there ſeemeth to be one *Cadency* or *Caſe* of the *firſt Declination,* of the *form Animate,* which endeth in *oh, uh,* or *ab*; viz. when an *animate Noun* followeth a *Verb tranſitive,* whoſe *object* that he acteth upon is *without himſelf.* For Example: *Gen.*1.16. the laſt word is *anogqſog,* ſtars. It is an *Erratum:* it ſhould be *anogqſoh*; becauſe it followeth the Verb *ayim,* He made. Though it.

8 *The* Indian *Grammar begun.*

Distrubutives ; as $\left\{\begin{array}{l}\text{Nawhutche, }some.\\ \text{Monaog, }many.\end{array}\right.$ $\left\{\begin{array}{l}\text{Tohsuog?}\\ \text{Tohsunash}\end{array}\right\}$ *How many?*

But because these are not of use in *affixing* to other *Parts of Speech*, they may as well be reckoned among *Adnouns*, as some do; though there is another *Schesis* upon them, and they attend upon *Verbs* as well as *Nouns*.

The *first* and *second persons* are of most use in affixing both of *Nouns* and *Verbs*, and other Parts of Speech.

The *third person singular* is affixed with such Syllables *as these*, Wut. wun. um. ∞. *& c.* having respect to *Euphonie:* And sometime the *third person*, especially of *Verbs*, hath no *affix*.

These *Pronouns*, (Neen *and* Ken) when they are affixed, they are *contracted into* Ne *and* Ke, and varied in the *Vocal* or *Vowel* according to *Euphonie*, with the word it is affixed unto ; *as* N∞, K∞, *& c.*

If the word unto which it is affixed begin with a *Vocal*, then a *Consonant* of a fitting sound is interposed, to couple the *word* and his *affix* with an Euphonie : *as* Nut. kut. num. kum, *& c.*

I give not *Examples* of these *Rules*, because they will be so obvious anon, when you see Nouns and Verbs *affixed*.

2. *Of a Noun.*

A *Noun* is a *Part of Speech* which signifieth *a thing* ; or it is the name *of a thing*.

The *variation* of Nouns is not by *Male* and *Female*, as in other Learned Languages, and in *European Nations* they do.

Nor are they *varied* by *Cases, Cadencies*, and *Endings* : herein they are more like to the *Hebrew*.

Yet there seemeth to be one *Cadency* or *Case* of the *first Declination*, of the *form Animate*, which endeth in *oh, uh*, or *ah* ; viz. when an *animate Noun* followeth a *Verb transitive*, whose *object* that he acteth upon is *without himself*. For Example: *Gen.1.16.* the last word is *anogqsog*, stars. It is an *Erratum* : it should be *anogqsoh* ; because it followeth the Verb *ayim*, He made. Though it be an *Erratum* in the Prefs, it is the fitter in fome refpects for an Example.

In *Nouns,* confider. $\begin{cases} 1. \textit{Genera,} \text{ or } \textit{kindes} \text{ of Nouns.} \\ 2. \text{ The } \textit{qualities} \text{ or } \textit{affections} \text{ thereof.} \end{cases}$

The *kindes* of Nouns are *two*; according to which there be *two Declenfions* of Nouns, for the variation of the number.

Numbers are two : *Singular* and *Plural.*

The firft *kinde* of Nouns is, when the *thing fignified* is *a living Creature.*

The fecond *kinde* is, when the *thing fignified* is *not a living creature.*

Therefore I order them thus :

There be *two forms* or *declenfions* of Nouns : $\begin{cases} \textit{Animate.} \\ \textit{Inanimate.} \end{cases}$

The *Animate form* or *declenfion* is, when the *thing fignified* is a living Creature : and fuch Nouns do alwayes make their Plural in (*og*); *as,* Wosketomp, *Man.* Wosketompaog. (*a*) is but for *Euphonie.* Mittamwoffis, *A Woman.* Mittamwoffiffog.

Nunkomp, *A young man.* Nunkompaog.

Nunkfqau, *A Girl.* Nunkfqauog.

Englifhman. Englifhmanog.

Englifhwoman. Englifhwomanog.

So Manit, *God.* Manittoog.

Mattannit, *The Devil.* Mattannittoog.

So Ox, Oxesog. Horfe, Horfesog.

The Stars they put in this form :

Anogqs, *A Star.* Anogqfog.

Muhhog, *The Body.* Muhhogkooog.

Pfukfes, *A little Bird.* Pfukfesog.

Ahtuk, *A Deer.* Ahtuhquog.

Mukquofhim, *A Wolf.* Mukquofhimwog.

Mofq, *A Bear.* Mofquog.

Tummunk, *The Beaver.* Tummunkquaog.

Puppinafhim, *A Beaft.* Puppinafhimwog.

Askook, *A Snake* or *Worm.* Askookquog.

Namohs, *A Fifh.* Namohfog. *&c.*

Some few Exceptions I know.

B 3 2. The

9 *The* Indian *Grammar begun.*

it be an *Erratum* in the Press, it is the fitter in some respects for an Example.

In *Nouns,* consider { 1. *Genera,* or *kindes* of Nouns.
2. The *qualities* or *affections* thereof.

The *kindes* of Nouns are *two*; according to which there be *two Declensions* of Nouns, for the variation of the number.

Numbers are two : *Singular* and *Plural.*

The first *kinde* of Nouns is, when the *thing signified is a living Creature.*

The second *kinde* is, when the *thing signified* is *not a living creature.*

Therefore I order them thus :

There be *two forms* or *declensions* of Nouns : { *Animate.*
Inanimate.

The *Animate form* or *declension* is, when the *thing signified* is a living Creature : and such Nouns do alwayes make their Plural in (*og*) ; as, Wosketomp, *Man.* Wosketompaog. (*a*) is but for *Euphonie.* Mittamwossis , *A Woman.* Mittamwossissog.

Nunkomp, *A young man.* Nunkompaog.

Nunksqau, *A Girl.* Nunksqauog.

Englishman. Englishmanog.

Englishwoman. Englishwomanog.

So Manit, *God.* Manittoog.

Mattannit, *The Devil.* Mattannittoog.

So Ox, Oxesog. Horse, Horsesog.

The Stars they put in this form :

Anogqs, *A Star.* Anogqsog.

Muhhog, *The Body.* Muhhogkooog.

Psukses, *A little Bird.* Psuksesog.

Ahtuk, *A Deer.* Ahtuhquog.

Mukquoshim, *A Wolf.* Mukquoshimwog.

Mosq, *A Bear.* Mosquog.

Tummunk, *The Beaver.* Tummunkquaog.

Puppinashim, *A Beast.* Puppinashimwog.

Askook, *A Snake* or *Worm.* Askookquog.

Namohs, *A Fish.* Namohsog. *&c.*

Some few Exceptions I know.

B 3

2. *The Inanimate form* or *declenfion* of Nouns, is when the *thing fignified* is not a living Creature: and thefe make the Plural in *afh* ; as

Huffun , *A Stone.* Huffunafh.
Quffuk, *A Rock.* Quffukquanafh.

Of this form are all Vegitables:
Mehtug, *A Tree.* Mehtugquafh.
Moskeht , *Grafs.* Moskehtuafh.

And of this form are all the parts of the Body: as
Muskefuk, *The Eye* or *Face.* Muskefukquafh.
Mehtauog, *An Ear.* Mehtauogwafh.
Meepit, *A Tooth.* Meepitafh.
Meenan, *The Tongue.* Meenanafh.
Muffiffittoon, *A Lip.* Muffiffiittoonafh.
Muttoon, *A Mouth.* Muttoonafh.
Menutcheg, *A Hand.* Menutchegafh.
Muhpit, *An Arm.* Muhpittenafh.
Muhkont, *A Leg.* Muhkontafh.
Muffeet, *The Foot.* Muffeetafh.

Of this form are all Virtues, and all Vices: as
Waantamoonk, *Wifdome.* Waantamooongafh, *or* onganafh.

All *Verbals* are of this *form,* which end in *onk,* and make their Plural in *ongafh,* or in *onganafh.*
All *Virtues* and *Vices* (fo far as at prefent I difcern) are *Verbals,* from their *activity* and *readinefs* to turn into *Verbs.*
All *Tools* and *Inftruments* of *Labour, Hunting, Fifhing, Fowling,* are of this *form.* All *Apparel, Houfing:* All *Fruits, Rivers, Waters, &c.*

So much for the kindes of Nounes.

The *common Affections* or *Qualifications* are two :
{ 1. The *affixing* of the *Noun* with the *Pronoun.*
{ 2. The *ranging* them into feveral *Ranks.*

1. The

2. *The Inanimate form* or *declension* of Nouns, is when the *thing signified* is not a living Creature: and these make the Plural in *ash* ; as
Hussun, *A Stone.* Hussunash.
Qussuk, *A Rock.* Qussukquanash.

Of this form are all Vegitables :
Mehtug, *A Tree.* Mehtugquash.
Moskeht, *Grass.* Moskehtuash.

And of this form are all the parts of the Body : as
Muskesuk, *The Eye* or *Face.* Muskesukquash.
Mehtauog, *An Ear.* Mehtauogwash.
Meepit, *A Tooth.* Meepitash.
Meenan, *The Tongue.* Meenanash.
Mussissittoon, *A Lip.* Mussissiittoonash.
Muttoon, *A Mouth.* Muttoonash.
Menutcheg, *A Hand.* Menutchegash.
Muhpit, *An Arm.* Muhpittenash.
Muhkont, *A Leg.* Muhkontash.
Musseet, *The Foot.* Musseetash.

Of this form are all Virtues, and all Vices : as
Waantamoonk, *Wisdome.* Waantamooongash, *or* onganash.

All *Verbals* are of this *form,* which end in *onk* , and make their Plural in *ongash,* or in *onganash.*

All *Virtues* and *Vices* (so far as at present I discern) are *Verbals,* from their *activity* and *readiness* to turn into *Verbs.*

All *Tools* and *Instruments* of *Labour, Hunting, Fishing, Fowling,* are of this *form.* All *Apparel, Housing :* All *Fruits, Rivers, Waters, &c.*

So much for the kindes of Nounes.

The common Affections or *Qualifications* are two :
{ 1. The *affixing* of the *Noun* with the *Pronoun.*
{ 2. The *ranging* them into several *Ranks.*

The way of *affixing* of Nouns, is the putting or ufing of the Noun in all the *three perfons*, both Singular and Plural.

This *manner of fpeech* being a new thing to us that know the *European* or Weftern Languages, it muft be demonftrated to us by *Examples.*

Metah *the Heart.*

Sing. { Nuttah, *my heart.* / Kuttah, *thy heart.* / Wuttah, *his heart.* }   Pl. { Nuttahhun, *our heart.* / Kuttahhou, *your heart.* / Wuttahhou, *their heart.* }

Menutcheg, *A Hand.*

Sing. { Nunnutcheg, *my hand.* / Kenutcheg, *thy hand.* / Wunnutcheg, *his hand.* }   Pl. { Nunnutcheganun, *our hand.* / Kenutcheganꝏ, *your hand.* / Wunnutcheganꝏ, *their hand.* }

Sing. { Nunnutcheganafh, *my hands.* / Kenutchegafh, or kenutcheganafh, *thy hands.* / Wunnutchegafh, or wunnutcheganafh, *his hands.* }

Plu. { Nunnutcheganunnonut, *our hands.* / Kenutcheganꝏwout, *your hands.* / Wunnutcheganꝏwout, *their hands.* }

Wétu, *A Houfe.*

Sing. { Neek, *my houfe.* / Keek, *thy houfe.* / Week, *his houfe.* }   Pl. { Neekun, *our houfe.* / Keekou, *your houfe.* / Weekou, *their houfe.* }

ut, in.

Sing. { Neekit, *in my houfe.* / Keekit, *in thy houfe.* / Weekit, *in his houfe.* }   pl. { Neekunonut, *in our houfe.* / Keekuwout, *in your houfe.* / Weekuwout, or wekuwomut, *in (his houfe.* }

Hence we corrupt this word Wigwam.

So much may at prefent fuffice for the affixing *of Nouns.*

Now

The way of *affixing* of Nouns, is the putting or using of the Noun in all the *three persons*, both Singular and Plural.

This *manner of speech* being a new thing to us that know the *European* or Western Languages, it must be demonstrated to us by *Examples.*

Metah, *the Heart.*

Sing. { Nuttah, *my heart.* Kuttah, *thy heart.* Wuttah, *his heart.* } *Pl.* { Nuttahhun, *our heart.* Kuttahhou, *your heart.* Wuttahhou, *their heart.*

Menutcheg, *A Hand.*

Sing. { Nunnutcheg, *my hand.* Kenutcheg, *thy hand.* Wunnutcheg, *his hand.* } *Pl.* { Nunnutcheganun, *our hand.* Kenutcheganoo, *your hand.* Wunnutcheganoo, *their hand.*

Sing. { Nunnutcheganash, *my hands.* Kenutchegash, *or* kenutcheganash, *thy hands.* Wunnutchegash, *or* wunnutcheganash, *his hands.*

Pl. { Nunnutcheganunnonut, *our hands.* Kenutcheganoowout, *your hands.* Wunnutcheganoowout, *their hands.*

Wétu, *A House.*

Sing. { Neek, *my house.* Keek, *thy house.* Week, *his house.* } *Pl.* { Neekun, *our house.* Keekou, *your house.* Weekou, *their house.*

ut, in.

Sing. { Neekit, *in my house.* Keekit, *in thy house.* Weekit, *in his house.* } *pl.* { Neekunonut, *in our house.* Keekuwout, *in your house.* Weekuwout, *or* wekuwomut, in (*his house.*

Hence we corrupt this word Wigwam.

So much may at present suffice for the affixing of Nouns.

Now for the ranging them into ranks.

There be *three Ranks* of Nouns ; { The *Primitive.*
{ The *Diminutive.*
{ The *Poſſeſſive.*

The ſame *Noun* may be uſed in all theſe *Ranks.*

The *primitive Rank* expreſſes the *the thing as it is* : *a* Nunkomp, *a Youth.* Nunkſqua, *a Girl.* Ox. Sheep. Horſe. Pig. *So* Haſſun, *a ſtone.* Mehtug, *a tree.* Moskeht, *graſs or herb.*

2. The *diminutive Rank* of Nouns doth *leſſen the thing*, and ex-preſſes it to be *a little one* ; and it is formed by *aading*, with a due Euphonie (*es*) or (*emes*) unto the *primitive Noun.* For Example, I ſhall uſe the ſame Nouns named in the *firſt Rank*, here in the ſecond *Rank* : *as* Nunkompaes *or* emes. Nunkſquaes *or* emes. Oxemes. Sheepſemes. Horſemes. Pigſemes. Haſſunemes. Meh-tugques, *or* Mehtugquemes. Moskehtuemes.

And ſo far as I perceive, theſe two endings (*es* and *emes*) are degrees of *diminution* : (*emes*) is the leaſt.

3. The *poſſeſſive Rank* of Nouns, is when the *perſon* doth chal-lenge an intereſt in the *thing.* Hence, as the other *Ranks* may be *affixed*, this muſt be *affixed with the Pronoun.*

And it is made by *adding the Syllable* (eum, *or* oom, *or* um) ac-cording to Euphonie, unto the affixed Noun. *For Example* : Num-Manittoom, *my God.* Nuttineneum, *my man.* Nunnunkomp-oom. Nunnunkſquaeum. Nutoxineum. Nusſheepſeum. Nut-horſesum. Nuppigsum. Nuthaſſunneum. Nummehtugkoom. Nummoskehteum. Nummoskehteumaſh.

Both the *primitive Noun*, and the *diminutive Noun*, may be uſed in the form *poſſeſſive* ; as *Nutſheepſemeſeum*, and the like.

Nouns may be turned into *Verbs* two wayes :

1. By turning the Noun into the Verb-ſubſtantive form : *as* Wosketompooo, *He became a man.* Of this ſee more in the *Verb Subſtantive.*

Now for the ranging them into ranks.

There be *three Ranks* of Nouns ; { The *Primitive.*
The *Diminutive.*
The *Possessive.*

The same *Noun* may be used in all these *Ranks.*

The *primitive Rank* expresses the *the thing as it is :* a Nunkomp, *a Youth.* Nunksqua, *a Girl.* Ox. Sheep. Horse. Pig. *So* Hassun, *a stone.* Mehtug, *a tree.* Moskeht, *grass* or *herb.*

2. The *diminutive Rank* of Nouns doth *lessen the thing,* and expresses it to be *a little one* ; and it is formed by *adding,* with a due Euphone (*es*) or (*emes*) unto the *primitive Noun.* For Example, I shall use the same Nouns named in the *first Rank ,* here in the *second Rank* : *as* Nunkomaes *or* emes. Nunksquaes *or* emes. Oxemes, Sheepsemes. Horsemes. Pigsemes. Hassunemes. Mehtugques, *or* Mehtugquemes. Moskehtuemes.

And so far as I perceive, these two endings (*es* and *emes*) are degrees of *diminution* : (*emes*) is the least.

3. The *possessive Rank* of Nouns, is when the *person* doth challenge an interest in the *thing.* Hence, as the other *Ranks* may be affixed, this must be *affixed with the Pronoun.*

And it is made by *adding the Syllable* (eum, *or* oom, *or* um) according to Euphonie, unto the affixed Noun. *For Example :* Num-Manittoom,   *my*   *God.*   Nuttineneum,   *my*   *man.* Nunnunkompoom.   Nunnunksquaeum.   Nutoxineum. Nussheepseum. Nuthorsesum. Nuppigsum. Nuthassunneum. Nummehtugkoom. Nummoskehteum. Nummoskehteumash.

Both the *primitive Noun,* and the *diminutive Noun,* may be used in the form *possessive* ; as *Nutsheepsemeseum,* and the like.

Nouns may be turned into *Verbs* two wayes :
1. By turning the Noun into the Verb-substantive form: *as* Wosketompoo, *He became a man.* Of this see more in the *Verb Substantive.*

2. All *Nouns* that end in *onk*, as they come from *Verbs* by adding (*onk*) so they will turn back again into *Verbs*, by taking away (*onk*) and forming the word according to the Rule of *Verbs*; as

Waantamoonk *is Wisdome:* take away *onk*, and then it may be *formed* Noowaantam, *I am wise.* Koowaantam, *Thou wise*, &c. Waantam, *He Wise*, &c.

3. *Of Adnouns.*

A N *Adnoun* is *a part of Speech* that *attendeth* upon a *Noun*, and signifieth *the Qualification* thereof.

The *Adnoun* is capable of both the *Animate* and *Inanimate forms*; and it agreeth with his *leading Noun*, in *form, number*, and *person*.

For Example: *Rev.* 4. 4. *there is* Neesneechagkodtash nabo yau appuongash, *Twenty four Thrones. And* Neesneechagkodtog yauog Eldersog, *Twenty four Elders.* Here be two *Nouns* of the two several forms, *Animate* and *Inanimate*; and the same *Adnoun* is made to agree with them both.

The *Inanimate form* of *Adnouns* end some in *i*, and some in *e*.

The *Animate form* in *es*, or *esu:* and those are turned into *Verbs*, by taking the *affix*. As

Wompi, *White.* Wompiyeuash.
Mooi, *Black.* Mooeseuash.
Menuhki, *Strong.* Menuhkiyeuash.
Noochumwi, *Weak.* Noochumwiyeuash.

The same Words in the Animate form:
Wompesu. Wompesuog.
Mooesu. Mooesuog.
Menuhkesu. Menuhkesuog.
Noochumwesu. Noochumwesuog.

Put the affix *to these, and they are Verbs.*

2. All *Nouns* that end in *onk*, as they come from *Verbs* by adding (*onk*) so they will turn back again into *Verbs*, by taking away (*onk*) and forming the word according to the Rule of *Verbs* ; as

Waantamoonk *is Wisdome :* take away *onk* , and then it may be *formed* Nꝏwaantam, *I am wise.* Kꝏwaantam, *Thou wise*, &c. Waantam, *He wise*, &c.

3. Of *Adnouns.*

AN *Adnoun* is a part *of Speech* that attendeth upon a *Noun*, and signifieth *the Qualification* thereof.

The *Adnoun* is capable of both the *Animate* and *Inanimate forms*, and it agreeth with his *leading Noun*, in *form, number*, and *person*.

For Example : *Rev.* 4. 4. *there is* Neesneechagkodtash nabo yau appuongash, *Twenty four Thrones. And* Neesneechagkodtog yauog Eldersog, *Twenty four Elders.* Here be two *Nouns* of the two several forms, *Animate* and *Inanimate* ; and the same *Adnoun* is made to agree with them both.

The *Inanimate form* of *Adnouns* end some in *i*, and some in *e*.

The *Animate form* in *es* , or *esu* : and those are turned into *Verbs*, by taking the *affix.* As

Wompi, *White.* Wompiyeuash.
Mꝏi, *Black.* Mꝏeseuash.
Menuhki, *Strong.* Menuhkiyeuash.
Nꝏchumwi, *Weak.* Nꝏchumwiyeuash.

The same words in the Animate form :
Wompesu. Wompesuog.
Mꝏesu. Mꝏesuog.
Menuhkesu. Menuhkesuog.
Nꝏchumwesu. Nꝏchumwesuog.

Put the affix to these, and they are Verbs.

NUmerals belong unto *Adnouns,* and in them there is some thing remarkable.

From the Number 5 and upward, they *adde a Word suppletive* which signifieth nothing, but receiveth the Grammatical variation of the *Declension,* according to the *things* numbered, *Animate* or *Inanimate.* The *Additional* is (*tohsú*) or (*tahshé*) which is varied (*tohsúog, tohsúash,* or *tohshinash.*)

For Example

1	*Nequt.*	6	*Nequtta tahshe.*
2	*Neese.*	7	*Nesausuk tahshe.*
3	*Nish.*	8	*Shwosuk tahshe.*
4	*Yau.*	9	*Paskoogun tahshe.*
5	*Napanna tahshe* {*tohsuog.* / *tohsuash.*}	10	*Piuk. Piukqussuog, Piuk-qussuash.*

Then from 10 to 20 they *adde* afore the Numeral (*nab* or *nabo*) and then it is not needful to *adde the following additional,* though sometimes they do it.

As for Example :

11	*Nabo nequt.*	16	*Nabo nequtta.*
12	*Nabo neese.*	17	*Nabo nesausuk.*
13	*Nabo nish.*	18	*Nabo shwosuk.*
14	*Nabo yau.*	19	*Nabo paskoogun.*
15	*Nabo napanna.*	20	*Neesneechag* {*kodtog.* / *kodtash.*}

Then *upwards* they *adde* to *Neesueechag,* the *single Numbers* to 30. *&c.*

30	*Nishwinchag*	*kodtog, kodtash*
40	*Yauunchag*	*kodtog, kodtash.*
50	*Napannatahshinchag*	*kodtog, kodtash.*
60	*Nequtta tahshinchag*	*kodtog, kodtash.*
70	*Nesausuk tahshinchag*	*kodtog, kodtash.*

80   *Shwosuk*

14 *The* Indian *Grammar begun.*

Numerals belong unto *Adnouns*, and in them there is some thing remarkable.

From the Number 5 and upward, they *adde a word suppletive* which signifieth nothing, but receiveth the Grammatical variation of the *Declension*, according to the *things* numbered, *Animate* or *Inanimate.* The *Additional* is (*tohsú*) or (*tahshé*) which is varied (*tohsúog, tohsúash,* or *tohshinash.*)

For Example

1	*Nequt.*	6	*Nequtta tahshe.*
2	*Neese.*	7	*Nesausuk tahshe.*
3	*Nish.*	8	*Shwosuk tahshe.*
4	*Yau.*	9	*Paskoogun tahshe.*
5	*Napanna tahshe* { *tohsuog.* *tohsuash.*	10	*Piuk. Piukqussuog, Piukqussuash.*

Then from 10 to 20 they *adde* afore the Numeral (*nab* or *nabo*) and then it is not needful to *adde the following additional,* though sometimes they do it.

As for Example :

11	*Nabo nequt.*	16	*Nabo nequtta.*
12	*Nabo neese.*	17	*Nabo nesausuk.*
13	*Nabo nish.*	18	*Nabo shwosuk.*
14	*Nabo yau.*	19	*Nabo paskoogun.*
15	*Nabo napanna.*	20	*Neesueechag* { *kodtog.* *kodtash.*

Then *upwards* they *adde* to *Neesueechag,* the *single Numbers* to 30. *&c.*

30	*Nishwinchag kodtog, kodtash.*
40	*Yauunchag kodtag, kodtash.*
50	*Napannatahshinchag kodtog, kodtash.*
60	*Nequtta tahshinchag kodtog, kodtash.*
70	*Nesausuk tahshinchag kodtog, kodtash.*

80 *Shwofuk tahſhinchag kodtog,   kodtaſh.*
90 *Paskoogux tahſhinchag kodtog,   kodtaſh.*
100 *Nequt paſuk* kꝏog, kꝏaſh.

1000 *Nequt muttannonganog* $\begin{Bmatrix} kodtog \\ kodtaſh. \end{Bmatrix}$ or $\begin{Bmatrix} kuſſuog. \\ kuſſuaſh. \end{Bmatrix}$

The *Adnoun* is frequently *compounded* with the *Noun,* and then
uſually they are *contracted: as*

    Womposketomp, *A white man.*
    Mꝏosketomp, *A black man.*
    Menuhkoſhketomp, *A ſtrong man.*
    Menuhkekont, *A ſtrong Leg.*   Qunuhtug, *of* qunni, *long.*
    Mehtug, *Wood* or *Tree.* And this word is uſed for *a Pike.*

When the *Noun* becometh a *Verb,* then the *Adnoun* becometh an
Adverb.

There is no form of *compariſon* that I can yet finde, but *degrees*
are expreſſed by a word ſignifying *more: as* Anue menuhkeſu,
More ſtrong: And Nano, *More and more.* Mꝏcheke, *Much.*
Peeſik *or* Peaſik, *Small.*

4. *Of the Verb.*

A *Verb* is when *the thing ſignified* is an *Action.*

There be two ſorts of Verbs.   The *Verb* $\begin{cases} Subſtantive. \\ Active. \end{cases}$

The *Verb Subſtantive,* is when any thing hath *the ſignification
of the Verb Subſtantive added to it :* as (*am, art, is, are, was,
were*) &c. *Actuall being* is above the nature of a *Noun,* and beneath the nature of a *Verb Active.*

We have no *compleat diſtinct word* for the *Verb Subſtantive,* as
other *Learned Languages,* and our *Engliſh Tongue* have, but it is
under a *regular compoſition,* whereby *many words* are made *Verb
Subſtantive.*

All

15 *The* Indian *Grammar begun.*

90   *Paskoogun tahshinchag kodtog, kodtash.*
100   *Nequt pasuk* kɔoog, kɔoash.
1000   *Nequt mutt annonganog* { *kodtog* / *kodtash.* } or { *kussuog.* / *kussuash.* }

The *Adnoun* is frequently *compounded* with the *Noun*, and then usually they are *contracted* : as

Womposketomp, *A white man.*
Mɔoosketomp, *A black man.*
Menuhkoshketomp, *A strong man.*
Menuhkekont, *A strong Leg.* Qunuhtug, *of* qunni, *long.*
Mehtug, *Wood* or *Tree.* And this word is used for *a Pike.*

When the *Noun* becometh a *Verb*, then the *Adnoun* becometh an *Adverb.*

There is no form of *comparison* that I can yet finde, but *degrees* are expressed by a word signifying *more* : as Anue menuhkesu, *More strong* : *And* Nano, *More and more.* Mɔocheke, *Much.* Peesik *or* Peasik, *Small.*

4. *Of the Verb.*

A *Verb* is when *the thing signified* is an *Action.*

There be two sorts of Verbs. The *Verb* { *Substantive.* / *Active.* }

The *Verb Substantive,* is when any thing hath *the signification of the Verb Substantive added to it* : as (*am, art, is, are, was, were*) &c. *Actuall being* is above the nature of a *Noun,* and beneath the nature of a *Verb Active.*

We have no *compleat distinct word* for the *Verb Substantive,* as other *Learned Language,* and our *English Tongue* have, but it is under a *regular composition,* whereby *many words* are made *Verb Substantive.*

All may be referred to *three forts,* fo far as yet I fee.

1. The *firft fort* of *Verb Subftantives* is made *by adding any of thefe Terminations to the word,* yeuꝏ, aꝏ, oꝏ ; with due *Euphonie :* And this is fo, be the word a *Noun* ; *as* Wosketompoꝏ, *He is a man :* Or *Adnoun* ; as Wompiyeuꝏ, *It is white :* Or be the word an *Adverb,* or the like ; as *James* 5.12. Mattayeuꝏutch, *Let it be nay :* Nuxyeuꝏutch, *Let it be yea.* The *words in the Text* are fpelled with refpeꝗt to *pronunciation,* more then to *Grammaticall compofition :* here I fpell them with refpeꝗt to *Grammaticall compofition.* See more Examples of this, *Exod.* 4. 3,4,6,7.

2. The *fecond fort* of *Verb Subftantives* is when the *animate Adnoun* is made *the third perfon of the Verb,* and fo *formed as a Verb : as* Wompefu, *white* ; Menuhkefu, *Strong* ; may be *formed as a Verb :* Nꝏwompes, Kꝏwompes, Wompefu. *And fo the like words.*

And of *this fort* are all *Adnouns of Vertue* or *Vice : as* Waantam, *wife :* Aſſꝏtu, *Foolifh,* &c.

Whatever is *affirmed to be,* or *denied to be,* or if it be *asked if it be,* or expreſſed to be *made to be* ; All *fuch words* may be *Verb Subftantives.* I fay, *may be,* becaufe there be *other wayes* in the Language to exprefs fuch a fenfe by. But it *may be thus.*

3. The *third fort,* are *Verb Subftantive paſſive,* when the *Verb Subftantive* (*am, is, was,* &c.) is fo annexed to a *Verb Aꝗtive,* that the *perfon affixed* is the *objeꝗt of the aꝗt* ; *as* Nꝏwadchanit, *I am kept.*

So much for the Verb Subftantive.

Now followeth the Verb Aꝗtive.

A *Verb Aꝗtive* is when the word fignifieth *a compleat aꝗtion,* or a *caufall power exerted.*

Verbs inceptives, or *inchoatives,* I finde not ; fuch a *notion* is expreſſed by *another word added to the Verb ,* which fignifieth *to begin,* or *to be about to do it.*

Alfo when the Aꝗtion is *doubled,* or *frequented,* &c. this *notion* hath

All may be referred to *three sorts*, so far as yet I see.

1. The *first sort* of *Verb Substantives* is made *by adding any of these Terminations to the word*, yeuωo, aωo, oωo ; with due *Euphonie* : And this is so, be the word a *Noun* ; *as* Wosketompoωo, *He is a man :* Or *Adnoun,* as Wompiyeuωo, *It is white :* Or be the word an *Adverb,* or the like ; as *James* 5. 12. Mattayeuωoutch, *Let it be nay :* Nuxyeuωoutch, *Let it be yea.* The *words in the Text* are spelled with respect to *pronunciation,* more then to *Grammaticall composition*: here I spell them with respect to *Grammaticall composition.* See more Examples of this, *Exod.* 4.3,4,6,7.

2. The *second sort of Verb Substantives* is when the *animate Adnoun* is made *the third person of the Verb,* and so *formed as a Verb*: as Wompesu, *White* ; Menuhkesu, *Strong* ; may be *formed as a Verb:* Nωowompes, Kωowompes, Wompesu. *And so the like words.*

And of *this sort* are all *Adnouns of Vertue* or *Vice : as* Waantam, *Wise* : Assωotu, *Foolish,* &c.

Whatever is *affirmed to be,* or *denied to be,* or if it be *asked if it be,* or expressed to be *made to be* ; All *such words* may be *Verb Substantives.* I say, *may be,* because there be *other wayes* in the Language to express such a sense by. But it *may be thus.*

3. The *third sort,* are *Verb Substantive passive,* when the *Verb Substantive* (*am, is, was,* &c.) is so annexed to a *Verb Active,* that the *person affixed* is the *object of the act* ; as Nωowadchanit, *I am kept.*

So much for the Verb Substantive.

Now followeth the Verb Active.

A *Verb Active* is when the *word* signifieth a *compleat action,* or a *causall power exerted.*

Verbs inceptives, or *inchoatives,* I finde not ; such a *notion* is expressed by *another word added to the Verb,* which signifieth *to begin,* or *to be about to do it.*

Also when the Action is *doubled,* or *frequented,* &c. this *notion* hath not a *diſtinct form*, but is expreſſed by *doubling the firſt Syllable* of the *word: as* Mohmoeog, *they oft met* ; Saſabbath-dayeu, :*very Sabbath.*

There be *two ſorts* or *forms* of *Verbs Active :*

{ 1. The *Simple form.*
{ 2. The *Suffix form.*

The *Simple form* of the *Verb Active,* is when the *act is converſant* about a *Noun inanimate* onely : *as*
  Noowadchanumun neek, *I keep my houſe.*
And this *Verb* may take the *form* of an *Adnoun : as*
  Noowadchanumunaſh noowéatchimineaſh, *I keep my corn.*
Or every *perſon* of this *Verb,* at leaſt in the *Indicative Mode,* will admit the *plural Number* of the *Noun inanimate.*
The *Suffix form* of the *Verb Active,* is when the *act is converſant* about *animate Nouns* onely ; or about both *animate* and *inanimate* alſo : *as*
  Koowadchanſh, *I keep thee.*
  Koowadchanumouſh, *I keep it for thee.*

There be *five Concordances* of the *Suffix form Active,* wherein the Verb doth receive a *various formation.* I think there be ſome more, but I have beat out no more.
The reaſon why I call them *Concordances,* is, Becauſe the *chief weight* and *ſtrength* of the *Syntaxis* of this Language, lyeth in this eminent manner of *formation of Nouns* and *Verbs,* with the *Pronoun perſons.*
  1. The *firſt Concordance* is, when the *object of the act* is an *animate Noun.* I call it, *The Suffix animate object : as*
  Koowadchanſh, *I keep thee.*
  2. The *Suffix animate mutual :* when *animates* are each others *object* ; *as*
  Noowadchanittimun, *we keep each other.*   This form ever wanteth the *ſingular Number.*
  3. The *Suffix animate end,* and *inanimate object : as*
  Koowadchanumouſh, *I keep it for thee* ; or, *for thy uſe.*
C 3   4. The

hath not a *distinct form*, but is expressed by *doubling the first Syllable* of the *word : as* Mohmoeog, *they oft met* ; Sasabbath-dayeu, *every Sabbath.*

       There be *two sorts* or *forms* of *Verbs Active :*

{ 1. The *Simple form.*
{ 2. The *Suffix form.*

    The *Simple form* of the *Verb Active*, is when the *act is conversant* about a *Noun inanimate* onely: *as*

        Nꝏwadchanumun neek, *I keep my house.*

And this *Verb* may take the form of an *Adnoun : as*

        Nꝏwadchanumunash nowéatchimineash, *I keep my corn.*

    Or every *person* of this *Verb*, at least in the *Indicative Mode*, will admit the *plural Number* of the *Noun inanimate.*

    The *Suffix form* of the *Verb Active*, is when the *act is conversant* about *animate Nouns* onely ; or about both *animate* and *inanimate* also : *as*

        Kꝏwadchansh, *I keep thee.*

        Kꝏwadchanumoush, *I keep it for thee.*

    There be *five Concordances* of the *Suffix form Active*, wherein the Verb doth receive a *various formation.* I think there be some more, but I have beat out no more.

    The reason why I call them *Concordances*, is, Because the *chief weight* and *strength* of the *Syntaxis* of this Language, lyeth in this eminent manner of *formation of Nouns* and *Verbs*, with the *Pronoun persons.*

    1. The *first Concordance* is, when the *object of the act* is an *animate Noun.* I call it, *The Suffix animate object : as*

        Kꝏwadchansh, *I keep thee.*

    2. The *Suffix animate mutual :* when *animates* are each others *object* ; *as*

        Nꝏwadchanittimun, *we keep each other.* This *form ever* wanteth the *singular Number.*

    3. The *Suffix animate end*, and *inanimate object : as*

        Kꝏwadchanumoush, *I keep it for thee*, or, *for thy use.*

4. The *Suffix animate form social* : *as*
     Kꝏweechewadchanumwomſh,   *I keep it with thee.*

5. The *Suffix form* advocate, or *in* ſtead *form*, when one acteth in the *room* or ſtead of another : *as*
     Kꝏwadchanumwanſhun ,   *I keep it for thee* ; *I act in thy ſtead.*

This *form* is of great uſe in *Theologie*, to expreſs what Chriſt *hath done for us* : *as*

     Nunnuppꝏwonuk,   *He died for me.*
     Kenuppꝏwonuk,   *He died for thee.*
     Kenuppꝏwonukqun,   *He died for us.*
     Kenuppꝏwonukꝏ,   *He died for you.*   &c.

All theſe forenamed *forms of Verbs*, both *Verb Subſtantives*, and *Verbs Active*, both *Simple* and *Suffix*, may be *varied* under three *diſtinct forms of variation* ; viz.

       ⎰ *Affirmative* : when the *act* is *affirmed.*
       ⎱ *Negative* : when the *act* is *denied.*
       ⎰ *Interrogative* : when the *act* is *queſtion'd.*

Again, many of theſe *forms* may alſo be varied in a *form cauſa-tive*, in all caſes where the *efficient* is capable to be *compelled*, or *cauſed to act.*

All theſe will be more conſpicuous in the *Paradigms*, or *Ex-amples.*

To make *compleat work* , I ſhould ſet down many Examples.

But I ſhall (at preſent) ſet down onely two Examples : One of the *Simple form Active* , which may generally ſerve for all the *Verb Subſtantives.*

The *ſecond Example* of the *Suffix animate form*, which may generally ſerve for all the *Concordances* of *Verbs ſuffixed.* Even as the *Meridian* of *Boſton* may generally ſerve for all *New-England* : And the *Meridian* of *London* may generally ſerve for all *England.*

And theſe will be enough to buſie the heads of *Learners* for a while.   Note

4. The *Suffix animate form social : as*
Kooweechewadchanumwomsh, *I keep it with thee.*

5. The *Suffix form advocate,* or *in stead form,* when one acteth in
the *room* or *stead* of another : as
Koowadchanumwanshun, *I keep it for thee* ;
I act in thy stead.

This *form* is of great use in *Theologie,* to express what Christ *hath
done for us : as*
Nunnuppoowonuk, *He died for me.*
Kenuppoowonuk, *He died for thee.*
Kenuppoowonukqun, *He died for us.*
Kenuppoowonukoo, *He died for you.* &c.

All these fore named *forms of Verbs,* both *Verb Substantives,* and
Verbs Active, both *Simple* and *Suffix,* may be *varied* under three *distinct forms of variation* ; viz.

{ *Affirmative :* when the *act* is *affirmed.*
Negative : when the *act* is *denied.*
Interrogative : when the *act* is *question'd.*

Again, many of these *forms* may also be varied in a *form
causative,* in all cases where the *efficient* is capable to be *compelled,* or
caused to act.

All these will be more conspicuous in the *Paradigms,* or
Examples.

To make *compleat work,* I should set down many Examples.

But I shall (at present) set down onely two Examples : One of
the *Simple form Active,* which may generally serve for all the *Verb
Substantives.*

The *second Example* of the *Suffix animate form,* which may generally serve for all the *Concordances* of *Verbs suffixed.* Even as the
Meridian of Boston may generally serve for all *New-England:* And
the *Meridian of London* may generally serve for all *England.*

And these will be enough to busie the heads of *Learners* for a
while.

Note this, That *all Verbs* cannot be formed through *all thefe forms,* but fuch Verbs as in reafon of Speech are *ufeable all thefe wayes,* which fundry Verbs are not ; as, *I fleep, eat, pifs,* &c.

Before I come to the *Paradigms,* there be other general Confiderations about *Verbs.*

In *Verbs* confider
{
1. Divers *Modes* of the *action.*
2. Divers *Times* of the *action.*
}

Firft, The *Modes of actions* in this Language are *five.*

1. The *Indicative, Demonftrative,* or *Interrogative Mode,* which doth fully *affert the action,* or *deny it,* or *enquire* if it be afferted :

As
{
Noowadchanumun, *I do keep it.*
Noowadchanumooun, *I do not keep it.*
Noowadchanumunas, *Do I keep it ?*
}

2. The *Imperative,* or *Hortative,* or *Praying* and *Bleffing Mode* is when the *action* is *Commanded,* or *Exhorted to be done,* or *Prayed* for. When a Superiour fpeaks in this *Mode,* he *commands.* When an Inferiour fpeaks in this *Mode,* he *prayes* and *intreats.* When a Minifter fpeaks in this *Mode,* he *exhorts,* and *bleffeth.*

Wadchanfh, *Keep thou.*
Wadchanch, *Keep me.*

3. The *Optative, Wifhing,* or *Defiring Mode,* when one defireth the *action to be done* : *as*

Noowaadchanumun toh, *I wifh* or *defire to keep it.*

4. The *Subjunctive,* or rather *the Suppofing,* or *Suppofitive Mode,* when the *action* is onely *fuppofed to be* ; as in thefe three expreffions :

{
If it be.
When it is.
It being.
}

And this third *fenfe* and *meaning* of this *Mode* of the Verb, doth turn this *Mode* into a *Participl,* like an *Adnoun,* very frequently.

5. The

Note this, That *all Verbs* cannot be formed through *all these forms*, but such Verbs as in reason of Speech are *useable all these wayes*, which sundry Verbs are not ; as, *I sleep, eat, piss*, &c.

Before I come to the *Paradigms*, there be other general Considerations about *Verbs*.

In *Verbs* consider
{
1. Divers *Modes* of the *action*.

2. Divers *Times* of the *action*.
}

First, The *Modes of actions* in this Language are *five*.

1. The *Indicative, Demonstrative*, or *Interrogative Mode*, which doth fully *assert the action*, or *deny it*, or *enquire* if it be asserted :

As
{
Nꝏwadchanumun, *I do keep it.*

Nꝏwadchanumꝏun, *I do not keep it.*

Nꝏwadchanumunas, *Do I keep it?*
}

2. The *Imperative*, or *Hortative*, or *Praying* and *Blessing Mode* is when the *action is Commanded*, or *Exhorted to be done*, or *Prayed* for. When a Superiour speaks in this *Mode*, he *commands*. When an Inferiour speaks in this *Mode*, he *prayes* and *intreats*. When a Minister speaks in this *Mode*, he *exhorts*, and *blesseth*.

Wadchansh, *Keep thou.*
Wadchanch, *Keep me.*

3. The *Optative, Wishing*, or *Desiring Mode*, when one desireth the *action to be done : as*

Nꝏwaadchanumun toh, *I wish* or *desire to keep it.*

4. The *Subjunctive*, or rather the *Supposing*, or *Suppositive Mode*, when the *action* is onely *supposed to be* ; as in these three expressions:

{
If it be.

When it is.

It being.
}

And this third *sense* and *meaning* of this *Mode* of the Verb, doth turn this *Mode* into a *Participle*, like an *Adnoun*, very frequently.

5. The *Indefinite Mode*, which doth onely aſſert the action with-out *limitation* of *perſon* or *time* ; and it is made of the *Indicative Mode*, by adding the termination (*át*) and taking away the *ſuffix* : as

Wadchanumunat, *To keep.*

There is another *Mode of the Verb* in reaſon of ſpeech, and in ſome other Languages, *viz.* The *Potential*, which doth render the action in *a poſſibility to be.* But this Language hath not ſuch a *Mode*, but that *notion* is expreſſed by a word ſignifying (*may*) to the *Indicative Mode.* The uſual word with us is (*woh*) *may* or *can.*

All theſe *Modes of the Verb* are *timed* by *Tenſes*, ſaving the *Inde-finite Mode*, and that is *unlimited.*

The *times* are two ; *Preſent*, and *Paſt.* The *time to come* is ex-preſſed by a word ſignifying *futurity*, added to the *Indicative Mode*, as (mos, piſh, *ſhall*, or *will*.)

In the *Roman Language* there do belong unto this *Indefinite Mode*, gerundive, *lofty*, and *vapouring* Expreſſions ; alſo *ſupine*, *ſluggiſh*, *dull*, and *ſunk-hearted* Expreſſions. And though the ſpi-rit of this People, *viz.* the *vapouring pride* of ſome, and the *dull-hearted ſupinity* of others, might diſpoſe them to ſuch words and expreſſions, yet I cannot finde them out.

As *Nouns* are often turned into *Verbs*, ſo *Verbs* are often turned into *Nouns* ; and a frequent way of it is, by adding (*onk*) to the *Verb* : as

Nꝏwompes, *I am white.*
Kꝏwompes, *Thou art white.*
Nꝏwompeſuonk, *My whiteneſs.*
Kꝏwompeſuonk, *Thy whiteneſs.*

Every *perſon of the Verb* that is capable of ſuch a *change* in the reaſon of Speech, may ſo be turned into a *Noun* ſingular or plural.

Before I ſet down the Examples of *Formation of Verbs*, I will finiſh *a few Obſervations* about the remaining Parts of Speech.

5. The *Indefinite Mode*, which doth onely assert the action without *limitation* of *person* or *time* ; and it is made of the *Indicative Mode*, by adding the termination (*át*) and taking away the *suffix* : as

Wadchanumunat, *To keep.*

There is another *Mode of the Verb* in reason of speech, and in some other Languages, *viz.* The *Potential*, which doth render the action in a *possibility to be.* But this Language hath not such a *Mode*, but that *notion* is expressed by a word signifying (*may*) to the *Indicative Mode.* The usual word with us is (*woh*) *may* or *can.*

All these *Modes of the Verb* are *timed* by *Tenses*, saving the *Indefinite Mode*, and that is *unlimited.*

The *times* are two ; *Present,* and *Past.* The *time* to *come* is expressed by a word signifying *futurity*, added to the *Indicative Mode*, as (mos, pish, *shall,* or *will.*)

In the *Roman Language* there do belong unto this *Indefinite Mode, gerundive, lofty,* and *vapouring* Expressions ; also *supine, sluggish, dull,* and *sunk-hearted* Expressions. And though the spirit of this People, *viz.* the *vapouring pride* of some, and *dull-hearted supinity* of others, might dispose them to such words and expressions, yet I cannot finde them out.

As *Nouns* are often turned into *Verbs,* so *Verbs* are often turned into *Nouns* ; and a frequent way of it is, by adding (*onk*) to the *Verb: as*

Noowompes, *I am white.*
Koowompes, *Thou art white.*
Noowompesuonk, *My whiteness.*
Koowompesuonk, *Thy whiteness.*

Every *person of the Verb* that is capable of such a *change* in the reason of Speech, may so be turned into a *Noun* singular or plural.

Before I set down the Examples of *Formation of Verbs,* I will finish *a few Observations* about the remaining Parts of Speech.

4. *Of Adverbs.*

AN *Adverb* is a word that *attendeth* upon the Verb, and signifieth *the quality of the action,* by *Extension, Diminution, Rectitude, Curvation, Duration, Cessation,* &c. according to the various qualities of all sorts of actions.

Adverbs do usually end in (*e* or *u*), as *wame* or *wamu,* All: *Menuhke* or *menuhku,* Strongly.

The several sorts of *Adverbs* (according as Learned Grammarians have gathered them together) are

1. *Of Time.* Yeuyeu, *Now.* Wunnonkou, *Yesterday.* Saup, *To morrow.* Ahquompak, *When.* Paswu, *Lately.* Nôadtuk, *A long time.* Teanuk, *Presently.* Kuttumma, *Very lately.*

2. *Of Place.* Uttiyeu, *where.* Naut, *There.* Anomut, *within.* Woskeche, *without.* Onkoue, *Beyond.* Negonnu, *First.* Wuttât, *Behinde.*

3. *Of Order.* Negonnu, *First.* Nahohtôeu, *Second.* Nishwu, *Third,* &c.

4. *Of Asking.* Sun, Sunnummatta; *Is it?* or *Is it not?* Tohwutch, *why.*

5. *Of Calling.* Hoh. Chuh.

6. *Affirming.* Nux, *Yea.* Wunnamuhkut, *Truely.*

7. *Denying.* Matta, Matchaog, *No.* Also Mo *sometimes signifieth* Not. They have no *Adverbs* of *Swearing,* nor any *Oath,* that I can yet finde: onely we teach them to Swear before a Magistrate *By the great and dreadfull Name of the Lord.* The word we make for *swearing,* signifieth *to speak vehemently.*

8. *Of Exhorting* or *Encouraging.* Ehhoh, Hah.

9. *Of Forbidding.* Ahque, *Beware, Do not.*

10. *Of Wishing.* Woi, Napehnont, *Oh that it were.* Toh,

11. *Of Gathering together.* Moeu, *Together.* Yeu nogque, *This way-ward.* Ne nogque, *That way-ward.* Kesukquieu, *Heaven-ward.* Ohkeiyeu, *Earth-ward.*

12. *Of Choosing.* Anue, *More rather.* Teaogku, *Rather, unfinished.* Nahen, *Almost.* Asquam, *Not yet.*

D

13. *Of*

4. *Of Adverbs*

AN *Adverb* is a word that *attendeth* upon the Verb, and signifi-eth *the quality of the action,* by *Extension, Diminution, Rectitude, Curvation, Duration, Cessation,* &c. according to the various quali-ties of all sorts of actions.

Adverbs do usually end in (*e* or *u*), as *wame* or *wamu,* All : *Menuhke* or *menuhku,* Strongly.

The several sorts of *Adverbs* (according as Learned Grammarians have gathered them together) are

1. *Of Time.* Yeuyeu, *Now.* Wunnonkou, *Yesterday.* Saup, *Tomorrow.* Ahquompak, *When.* Paswu, *Lately.* Nôadtuk, *A long time.* Teanuk, *Presently.* Kuttumma, *Very lately.*

2. *Of Place.* Uttiyeu, *Where.* Naut, *There.* Anomut, *Within.* Woskeche, *Without.* Onkoue, *Beyond.* Negonnu, *First.* Wuttát, *Behinde.*

3. *Of Order.* Negonnu, *First.* Nahothôeu, *Second.* Nishwu, *Third,* &c.

4. *Of Asking.* Sun, Sunnummatta, *Is it ?* or *Is it not ?* Tohwutch, *Why.*

5. *Of Calling.* Hoh. Chuh.

6. *Affirming.* Nux, *Yea.* Wunnamuhkut, *Truely.*

7. *Denying.* Matta, Matchaog, *No. Also* Mo *sometimes signifieth* Not. They have no *Adverbs* of *Swearing,* nor any *Oath,* that I can yet finde : onely we teach them to Swear before a Magistrate *By the great and dreadfull Name of the Lord.* The word we make for *swear-ing,* signifieth *to speak vehemently.*

8. *Of Exhorting* or *Encouraging.* Ehhoh, Hah.

9. *Of Forbidding.* Ahque, *Beware, Do not.*

10. *Of Wishing.* Woi, Napehnont, *Oh that it were.* Toh.

11. *Of Gathering together.* Moeu, *Together.* Yeu nogque, *This way-ward.* Ne nogque, *That way-ward.* Kesukquieu, *Heaven-ward.* Ohkeiyeu, *Earth-ward.*

12. *Of Choosing.* Anue, *More rather.* Teaogku, *Rather, unfin-ished.* Nahen, *Almost.* Asquam, *Not yet.*

13. *Of Continuation.*   Aſh, *Still.*
14. *Of Shewing.*   Kuſſeh, *Behold.*
15. *Of Doubting.*   Pagwodche, *It may be.* Toh, *It may be.*
16. *Of Likeneſs.*   Netatup, *Like ſo.* Nemehkuh, *So.* Neane, *As.*
17. *Of unexpected Hap.*   Tiadche, *Unexpectedly.*
18. *Of Quality*   Wunnegen.   Matchet.   Waantamwe , *&c.*
      Of this kinde are all Virtues *and* Vices.   *&c.*

Adverbs are oft turned into *Adnouns*, eſpecially when his *Verb* is turned into a *Noun.*

6. *Of the Conjunction.*

A *Conjunction* is a Part of Speech to joyn *words* and *Sentences :*   As
Cauſatives.   Wutch, wutche , newutche.   *For , from , becauſe.*
Yeu waj, *For this cauſe.*
Disjunctives.   Aſuh, *Or.*
Diſcretives.   Qut, *But.*
Suppoſitives.   Tohneit, *If.*
Exceptives.   Iſhkont, *Leaſt.* Chaubohkioh, *Except,* or *beſides.*
Kuttumma, *Unleſs.*
Diverſatives.   Tohkônogque, *Although.*
Of Poſſibility.   Woh, *May* or *Can.*
Of Place.   In, en, ut, at. *In, At.* or *To.*

7. *Of Interjections.*

A N *Interjection* is a word, or ſound that uttereth the *paſſion of the minde* without dependance on other words.
Of Sorrow.   Woi, oowee.
Of Marvelling.   Hó, hoo
Of Diſdaining.   Quah.
Of Encouraging.   Hah, Ehoh.

There

22 *The* Indian *Grammar begun.*

13. *Of Continuation.* Ash, *Still.*
14. *Of Shewing.* Kusseh, *Behold.*
15. *Of Doubting.* Pagwodche, *It may be.* Toh, *It may be.*
16. *Of Likeness.* Netatup, *Like so.* Nemehkuh, *So* Neane, *As.*
17. *Of unexpected Hap.* Tiadche, *Unexpectedly.*
18. *Of Quality.* Wunnegen. Matchet. Waantamwe, *&c.*
Of this kinde are all Virtues *and Vices.* *&c.*

Adverbs are oft turned into *Adnouns*, especially when his *Verb* is turned into a *Noun.*

6. *Of the Conjunction.*

A *Conjunction is a* Part of Speech to joyn *Words* and *Sentences* : As
Causatives. Wutch, wutche, newutche. *For, from, because,*
Yeu waj, *For this cause.*
Disjunctives. Asuh, *Or.*
Discretives. Qut, *But.*
Suppositives. Tohneit, *If.*
Exceptives. Ishkont, *Least.* Chaubohkioh, *Except, or besides.*
Kuttumma, *Unless.*
Diversatives. Tohkônogque, *Although.*
Of Possibility. Woh, *May or Can.*
Of Place. In, en, ut, at. *In, At or To.*

7. *Of Interjections.*

A N *Interjection is a word or sound that uttereth the passion of the minde,* without dependance on other words.
Of Sorrow. Woi, oowee.
Of Marvelling. Hó, hoo.
Of Disdaining. Quah.
Of Encouraging. Hah, Ehoh.

There be alfo *fuppletive Syllables* of no fignification, but for *orna-ment* of the word : as *tit, tin, tinne* ; and thefe, in way of an *Ele-gancy*, receive the *affix* which belongeth to the *Noun* or *Verb* fol lowing ; as *nuttit, kuttit,* Wuttit, *nuttin, kuttin,* Wuttin, *nuttinne, kuttinne,* wuttinne.

Other Languages have their *fignificant fuppletives* for Elegancy : and fome of our Englifh Writers begin fo to ufe [*why*], but I con-ceive it to be a *miftake.*   Our *fuppletive* is rather [*weh*], and [*why*] is a *fignificant word.* It oft puts the Reader to this inconvenience, to ftay and look whether it be fignificant or not ; and fome are *ftum-bled* at it.   It is feldome *an Elegancy,* to make a fignificant word a meer fuppletive.

So much for the formation of words afunder.

For the Conftruction of words together, *I will give*
three fhort Rules.

1.   WHen *two Nouns come together,* one of them is turned into a kinde of an Adverb, or Adnoun, and that is an *Elegancy* in the Language : of which fee frequent Examples.   See 1 *Pet.*2.2. Pahke fogkodtungane wuttinnowaonk, *The pure milkie word,* for *Milk of the word.*   The like may be obferved a thoufand times.

2.   When *two Verbs come together,* the latter is the *Infinitive Mode* : as in the fame 1 *Pet.*2.5. Kooweekikonitteamwoo fephau-finat. *Ye are built,* &c. *to facrifice,* &c. And a thoufand times more this Rule occurs.

3.   When a *Noun* or a *Verb* is attended upon with an *Adnoun* or *Adverb,* the *affix* which belongeth to the Noun or Verb is *prefixed* to the Adnoun or Adverb : as in the fame Chapter, 1 *Pet.* 2.9. Ummonchanatamwe wequaiyeumut, *His marvellous light :* The affix of *Light* is prefixed to *marvellous.* Koowaantamwe ketooh-kam, *Thou fpeakeft wifely :* The affix of *fpeaking* is prefixed to *wifely.* This is a frequent Elegancy in the Language

But the manner of the *formation* of the *Nouns* and *Verbs* have fuch a *latitude of ufe,* that there needeth little other *Syntaxis* in the Language.   D 2   I fhall

There be also *suppletive Syllables* of no signification, but for *ornament* of the word : as *tit, tin, tinne* ; and these, in way of an *Elegancy*, receive the *affix* which belongeth to the *Noun* or *Verb* following ; as *nuttit, kuttit, wuttit, nuttin, kuttin, wuttin, nuttinne, kuttinne, wuttinne.*

Other Languages have their *significant suppletives* for Elegancy : and some of our English Writers begin so to use [*Why*], but I conceive it to be a *mistake.* Our *suppletive* is rather [*Weh*], and [*Why*] is a *significant word.* It oft puts the Reader to this inconvenience, to stay and look whether it be significant or not; and some are *stumbled* at it. It is seldome an *Elegancy*, to make a significant word a meer suppletive.

So much for the formation of words asunder.

For the Construction of words together, I will give three short Rules.

WHen *two Nouns come together*, one of them is turned into a kinde of an Adverb, or Adnoun, and that is an *Elegancy* in the Language : of which see frequent Examples. See 1 *Pet.*2.2. Pahkesogkodtungane wuttinnowaonk, *The pure milkie word*, for *Milk of the word.* The like may be observed a thousand times.

2. When *two Verbs come together*, the latter is the *Infinitive Mode:* as in the same 1 *Pet.*2.5. Kꝏweekikonitteamwꝏ sephausinat. *Ye are built*, &c. *to sacrifice*, &c. And a thousand times more this Rule occurs.

3. When a *Noun* or a *Verb* is attended upon with an *Adnoun* or *Adverb*, the *affix* which belongeth to the Noun or Verb is *prefixed* to the Adnoun or Adverb : as in the same Chapter, 1 *Pet.*2.9. Ummonchanatamwe wequaiyeumut, *His marvellous light :* The affix of *Light* is prefixed to *marvellous.* Kꝏwaantamwe ketꝏhkam, *Thou speakest wisely :* The affix of *speaking* is prefixed to *wisely.* This is a frequent Elegancy in the Language.

But the manner of the *formation* of the *Nouns* and *Verbs* have such a *latitude of use*, that there needeth little other. *Syntaxis* in the Language.

I fhall now fet down *Examples of Verbs :* and firft of the *Simple form.* And here

Firft, I fhall fet down a *Verb Active,* whofe object is *Inanimate :* as Noowadchanumun, *I keep it. (Be it tool or garment.)*
And fecondly, I fhall fet down a *Verb Subftantive :* as Noowaantam, *I am wife.*

Both thefe I fhall fet down *Parallel* in two Columes.

The form Affirmative.

Indicative Mode.

Prefent tenfe.		Prefent tenfe.	
	I keep it.		*I am wife.*
Sing.	Noowadchanumun Koowadchanumun oowadchanumun.	*Sing.*	Noowaantam Koowaantam Waantam noh.
Plur.	Noowadchanumumun Koowadchanumumwoo Wadchanúmwog.	*pl.*	Noowaantamumun Koowaantamumwoo Waantamwog.

Præter tenfe.		*Præter tenfe.*	
Sing.	Noowadchanumunap Koowadchanumunap oowadchanumunap.	*Sing.*	Noowaantamup Koowaantamup Waantamup.
Pl.	Noowadchanumumunnónup Koowadchanumumwop Wadchanumuppanneg : or oowadchanummuáop.	*pl.*	Noowaantamumunnónup Koowaantamúmwop Waantamuppanneg;

The *Imperative Mode,* when it *Commands* or *Exhorts* it wanteth the firft perfon *fingular :* but when we *Pray* in this *Mode,* as alwayes we do, then it hath the *firft* perfon ; as, *Let me be wife :* but there is no formation of the word to exprefs it ; yet it may be expreffed.

The Indian *Grammar begun.*

I shall now set down *Examples of Verbs* : and first of the *Simple form*. And here

First, I shall set down a *Verb Active*, whose object is *Inanimate: as* Noowadchanumun, *I keep it.* (*Be it tool* or *garment.*)

And secondly, I shall set down a *Verb Substantive: as* Noowaantam, *I am wise.*

Both these I shall set down *Parallel* in two Columes

The form Affirmative.

Indicative Mode.

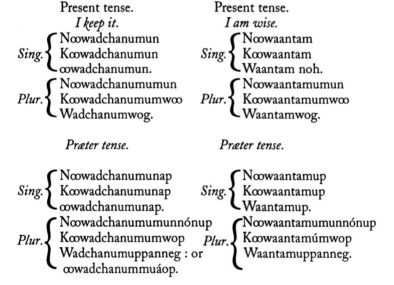

Present tense.
I keep it.

Sing. { Noowadchanumun
Koowadchanumun
oowadchanumun.

Plur. { Noowadchanumumun
Koowadchanumumwoo
Wadchanumwog.

Present tense.
I am wise.

Sing. { Noowaantam
Koowaantam
Waantam noh.

Plur. { Noowaantamumun
Koowaantamumwoo
Waantamwog.

Præter tense.

Sing. { Noowadchanumunap
Koowadchanumunap
oowadchanumunap.

Plur. { Noowadchanumumunnónup
Koowadchanumumwop
Wadchanumuppanneg : or
oowadchanummuáop.

Præter tense.

Sing. { Noowaantamup
Koowaantamup
Waantamup.

Plur. { Noowaantamumunnónup
Koowaantamúmwop
Waantamuppanneg.

The *Imperative Mode*, when it *Commands* or *Exhorts* it wanteth the *first person singular :* but when we *Pray* in this *Mode*, as always we do, then it hath the *first person* ; as, *Let me be wise :* but there is no formation of the word to express it; yet it may be expressed

preſſed by adding this word unto the *Indicative Mode* [pâ], *as*, Pânoowaantam, *Let me be* wiſe.   Our uſual formation of the *Imperative Mode* is without the *firſt perſon ſingular*, caſting away the
Aſſix.

Imperative Mode.

Preſent tenſe.	Preſent tenſe.
Sing. { VVadchaniſh VVadchanitch.	Sing. { VVaantaſh VVaantaj.
plur. { VVadchanumuttuh VVadchanumook VVadchanumahettich.	plur. { VVaantamuttuh VVaantamook VVaantamohettich.

The *Imperative Mode* cannot admit of any other *time* then the
Preſent.

The *Optative Mode.*

Preſent tenſe.	Preſent tenſe.
Sing. { Noowáadchánumun-toh Koowáadchanumun-toh oowaadchanumun-toh.	Sing. { Noowáaantamun-toh Koowáaantamun-toh oowáaantamun-toh.
plur. { Noowaadchanumunnan-toh Koowaadchanumunnan-toh oowaadchanumuneau-toh.	pl. { Noowáaantamunan-toh Koowáaantamuneau-toh oowáaantamuneau-toh.

Præter tenſe.	Præter tenſe.
Sing. { Noowaadchanumunaz-toh Koowaadchanumunaz-toh oowaadchanumunaz-toh	Sing. { Noowáaantamunaz-toh Koowáaantamunaz-toh oowáaantamunaz-toh.
pl. { Noowaadchanumunannonuz-toh Koowaadchanumunaóuz-toh oowaadchanumunnaóuz-toh.	pl. { Noowáaantamánanôiz-toh Koowáaantamunaóiz-toh oowáaantamunaóiz-toh

It ſeems their deſires are ſlow, *but* ſtrong ;
Becauſe they be utter'd double-breath't, *and* long.
D 3   The

by adding this word unto the *Indicative Mode* [pâ], *as,*
Pânoowaantam, *Let me be wise.* Our usual formation of the
Imperative Mode is without the *first person singular,* casting away the
Affix.

Imperative Mode

Present tense.

Sing. { Wadchanish
Wadchanitch.

plur. { Wadchanumuttuh
Wadchanumook
Wadchanumahettich.

Present tense.

Sing. { Waantash
Waantaj.

plur. { Waantamuttuh
Waantamook
Waantamohettich.

The *Imperative Mode* cannot admit of any other *time* then the
Present.

The *Optative Mode.*

Present tense.

Sing. { Noowáadchánumun-toh
Koowáadchanumun-toh
oowaadchanumun-toh

plur. { Noowaadchanumunnan-toh
Koowaadchanumunnan-toh
oowaadchanumuneau-toh.

Present tense.

Sing. { Noowáaantamun-toh
Koowáaantamun-toh
oowáaantamun-toh.

pl. { Noowáaantamunan-toh
Koowáaantamuneau-toh
oowáaantamuneau-toh.

Præter tense.

Sing. { Noowaadchanumunaz-toh
Koowaadchanumunaz-toh
oowaadchanumunaz-toh

pl. { Noowaadchanumunannonuz-toh
Koowaadchanumunaóuz-toh
oowaadchanumunnaóuz-toh.

Præter tense.

Sing. { Noowáaantamunaz-toh
Koowáaantamunaz-toh
oowáaantamunaz-toh.

pl. { Noowáaantamánanôiz-toh
Koowáaantamunaôiz-toh
oowáaantamunaôiz-toh.

It seems their desires are slow, *but* strong ;
Because they be utter'd double-breath't, *and* long.

The *Suppofitive Mode* : which ufually *flats* the *firft Vocal,* and layes by the *affix.*

Prefent tenfes			*Prefent tenfe.*		
Sing.	⎰ Wadchanumon		*Sing.*	⎰ Waantamon	
	⎱ Wadchanuman			⎱ Waantaman	
	Wadchanuk.			Waantog.	
plur.	⎰ VVadchanumog		*plur.*	⎰ VVaantamog	
	⎱ VVadchanumóg			⎱ VVaantamóg	
	VVadchanumahettir.			VVaantamohettit.	

Præter tenfe.		*Præter tenfe.*	
Sing.	⎰ VVadchanumos	*Sing.*	⎰ VVaantamos
	⎱ VVadchanumôfa		⎱ VVaantamas
	VVadchanukis.		VVaantogkis.
plur.	⎰ VVadchanumogkus	*plur.*	⎰ VVaantamogkis
	⎱ VVadchanumógkus		⎱ VVaantamógkis
	VVadchanumahettis.		VVaantamohettis.

The *Indefinite Mode.*

VVadchanumunát. VVaantamunát.

Indicative Mode. The *form Negative,* which is varied from the *Affirmative* by interpofing [∞].

Prefent tenfe.		*Prefent tenfe.*	
Sing.	⎰ Noowadchanumooun	*Sing.*	⎰ Noowaantamooh
	⎱ Koowadchanumooun		⎱ Koowaantamooh
	oowadchanumooun.		Waantamooh.
plur.	⎰ Noowadchanumoounnonup	*plur.*	⎰ Noowaantamoomun
	⎱ Koowadchanumoowop		⎱ Koowaantamoomwoo
	Wadchanumooog.		Waantamooog.

Præter tenfe		*Præter tenfe*	
Sing.	⎰ Noowadchanumoounap	*Sing.*	⎰ Noowaantamoop
	⎱ Koowadchanumoounap		⎱ Koowaantamoop
	oowadchanumoounap.		oowaantamop.
pl.	⎰ Noowadchanumoounnanónup	*plur.*	⎰ Noowaantamoomunnonup
	⎱ Koowadchanumoowop		⎱ Koowaantamoomwop
	Wadchanumoopanneg.		VVaantamoopanneg.

The

The *Suppositive Mode* : which usually *flats* the *first Vocal*, and layes by the *affix.*

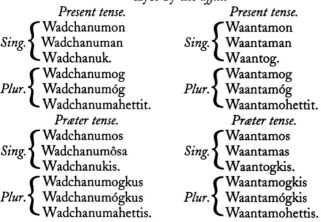

	Present tense.		*Present tense.*
Sing. {	Wadchanumon	*Sing.* {	Waantamon
	Wadchanuman		Waantaman
	Wadchanuk.		Waantog.
Plur. {	Wadchanumog	*Plur.* {	Waantamog
	Wadchanumóg		Waantamóg
	Wadchanumahettit.		Waantamohettit.
	Præter tense.		*Præter tense.*
Sing. {	Wadchanumos	*Sing.* {	Waantamos
	Wadchanumôsa		Waantamas
	Wadchanukis.		Waantogkis.
Plur. {	Wadchanumogkus	*Plur.* {	Waantamogkis
	Wadchanumógkus		Waantamógkis
	Wadchanumahettis.		Waantamohettis.

The *Indefinite Mode.*

Wadchanumunát.   Waantamunát.

Indicative Mode. The *form Negative,* which is varied from the *Affirmative* by interposing [oo].

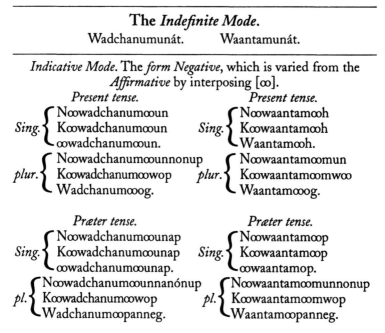

	Present tense.		*Present tense.*
Sing. {	Noowadchanumooun	*Sing.* {	Noowaantamooh
	Koowadchanumooun		Koowaantamooh
	oowadchanumooun.		Waantamooh.
plur. {	Noowadchanumoounnonup	*plur.* {	Noowaantamoomun
	Koowadchanumoowop		Koowaantamoomwoo
	Wadchanumooog.		Waantamooog.
	Præter tense.		*Præter tense.*
Sing. {	Noowadchanumoounap	*Sing.* {	Noowaantamoop
	Koowadchanumoounap		Koowaantamoop
	oowadchanumoounap.		oowaantamop.
pl. {	Noowadchanumoounnanónup	*pl.* {	Noowaantamoomunnonup
	Koowadchanumoowop		Koowaantamoomwop
	Wadchanumoopanneg.		Waantamoopanneg.

The *Imperative Mode* of the *Negative simple form.*

Present tense.

Sing. { VVadchanuhkon
{ VVadchanuhkitch

plur. { VVadchanumꝏuttuh
{ wadchanumꝏhteók
{ wadchanumohettekitch.

Present tense.

Sing. { VVaantukon
{ VVaantukitch

plur. { VVaantamꝏuttuh
{ waantamꝏhteók
{ waantamóhettekitch.

The *Optative Mode* is of seldome use, and very difficult, therefore I pass it by.

The *Suppositive Mode* of the *Simple form.*

Present tense.

Sing. { Wadchanumꝏun
{ Wadchanumꝏan
{ Wadchanꝏg.

Plur. { Wadchanumꝏóg
{ Wadchanumꝏóg
{ Wadchanumꝏahettit, *or* ꝏhetteg.

Present tense.

Sing { Waantamꝏon
{ Waantamꝏau
{ Waantamꝏg.

Pl. { Waantamꝏog
{ Waantamꝏóg
{ Waantamꝏohettit, *or* ꝏhetteg.

Præter tense.

Sing. { Wadchanumꝏos
{ Wadchanumꝏosa
{ Wadchanumꝏgkis.

Plur. { Wadchanumꝏogkus
{ Wadchanumꝏogkus
{ Wadchanumꝏahettis

Præter tense.

Sing. { Waantamꝏos
{ Waantamꝏas
{ Waantamꝏgkis

Plur. { Waantamꝏogkus
{ Waantamꝏógkus
{ Waantamꝏohettis.

The *Indefinite Mode* of the *Simple form Negative.*

Wanchanumꝏunát.   Waantamꝏunát.

The *Simple form Interrogative,* is formed onely in the *Indicative Mode :* All *Questions* are alwayes asked in this *Mode of the Verb,* and in no other ; and it is *formed* by adding [*ás*] to the *Affirmative.*

Indicative Mode

Present tense.

Sing. { Nꝏwadchanumunás.
{ Kꝏwadchanumunás.
{ ꝏwadchanumunáous.

Present tense.

Plur. { Nꝏwadchanumunnanonus.
{ Kꝏwadchanumunnaóus.
{ ꝏwadchanumunnaóus Nag.

The *Imperative Mode* of the *Negative simple form.*

	Present tense.		Present tense.
Sing.	{ Wadchanuhkon { Wadchanuhkitch	*Sing.*	{ Waantukon { Waantukitch
plur.	{ Wadchanumoouttuh { wadchanumoohteók { wadchanumohettekitch.	*plur.*	{ Waantamoouttuh { waantamoohteók { waantamóhettekitch.

The *Optative Mode* is of seldome use, and very difficult, therefore I pass it by.

The *Suppositive Mode* of the *Simple form.*

	Present tense.		Present tense.
Sing.	{ Wadchanumooun { Wadchanumooan { Wadchanoog.	*Sing.*	{ Waantamooon { Waantamooan { Waantmoog.
Plur.	{ Wadchanumooóg { Wadchanumooóg { Wadchanumooahettit, *or* oohetteg.	*Plur.*	{ Waantamooog { Waantamooóg { Waantamooohettit, or oohetteg.

	Præter tense.		Præter tense.
Sing.	{ Wadchanumooos { Wadchanumooosa { Wadchanumoogkis.	*Sing.*	{ Waantamooos { Waantamooas { Waantamoogkis.
Plur.	{ Wadchanumooogkus { Wadchanumooógkus { Wadchanumooahettis.	*Plur.*	{ Waantamooogkus { Waantamooógkus { Waantamooohettis.

The *Indefinite Mode* of the *Simple form Negative.*
Wanchanumoounát.   Waantamoounát.

The *Simple form Interrogative,* is formed onely in the *Indicative Mode* : All *Questions* are alwayes asked in this *Mode of the Verb,* and in no other ; and it is *formed* by adding [*ás*] to the *Affirmative.*

Indicative Mode.

	Present tense.		Present tense.
Sing.	{ Noowadchanumunás. { Koowadchanumunás. { oowadchanumunáous.	*Plur.*	{ Noowadchanumunnanonus. { Koowadchanumunnáous. { oowadchanumunnáous. Nag.

The *Suffix form animate Affirmative.*

Here I carry in a Parallel our English *Verb* (Pay) that so any may distinguish betwixt what is Grammar, and what belongs to the word.   And remember ever to pronounce (pay), because else you will be ready to reade it (pau).   Also remember, that (Paum) is the radicall word, and all the rest is Grammar.   In this remarkable way of speech, the Efficient of the Act, and the Object, and sometimes the End also, are in a regular composition comprehended in the Verb : and there is no more difficulty in it, when use hath brought our Notion to it, then there is in other Languages, if so much.

Indicative Mode. Prefent tenfe.

1 *sing.*
- *I keep thee,* Koowadchanſh.
- *I keep him,* Noowadchan.
- *I keep you,* Koowadchanunumwoo.
- *I keep them,* Noowadchanóog.

1 plur.
- *I pay thee,* Kuppaumuſh.
- *I pay him,* Nuppayum.
- *I pay you,* Kuppaumunumwoo.
- *I pay them,* Nuppaumôog.

2 *sing.*
- *Thou keepeſt me,* Koowadchaneh.
- *Thou keepeſt him,* Koowadchan.
- *Thou keepeſt us,* Koowadchanimun.
- *Thou keepeſt them,* Koowadchanoog.

2 plur.
- *Thou payeſt me,* Kuppaumeh.
- *Thou payeſt him,* Kuppaum.
- *Thou payeſt us,* Kuppaumimun.
- *Thou payeſt them,* Kuppaumoog.

3 *sing.*
- *He keepeth me,* Noowadchanuk.
- *He keepeth thee,* Koowadchanuk.
- *He keepeth him,* oowadchanuh.
- *He keepeth us,* Koowadchanukqun.
- *He keepeth you,* Koowadchanukoo.
- *He keepeth them,* oowadchanuh.

3 plur.
- *He payeth me,* Nuppaumuk.
- *He payeth thee,* Kuppaumuk.
- *He payeth him,* Uppaumuh.
- *He payeth us,* Kuppaumukqun.
- *He payeth you,* Kuppaumukou.
- *He payeth them,* Uppaumuh nah.

The

28 *The* Indian *Grammar begun.*

The *Suffix form animate Affirmative.*

Here I carry in a Parallel our English Verb (Pay) *that so any may distingwish betwixt what is Grammar, and what belongs to the word. And remember ever to pronounce* (pay), *because else you will be ready to reade it* (pau). *Also remember that* (Paum) *is the radicall word and all the rest is Grammar. In this remarkable way of speech, the Efficient of the Act, and the Object, and sometimes the End also, are in a regular composition comprehended in the Verb : and there is no more difficulty in it, when use hath brought our Notion to it, then there is in other Languages, if so much.*

Indicative Mode, Present tense.

1 sing.
I *keep thee,*
Koowadchansh.
I *keep him,*
Noowadchan.
I *keep you,*
Koowadchanunumwoo.
I *keep them,*
Noowadchanóog.

1 plur.
I *pay thee,*
Kuppaumush.
I *pay him,*
Nuppayum.
I *pay you,*
Kuppaumunumwoo.
I *pay them,*
Nuppaumôog.

2 sing.
Thou keepest me,
Koowadchaneh.
Thou keepest him,
Koowadchan.
Thou keepest us,
Koowadchanimun.
Thou keepest them,
Koowadchanoog.

2 plur.
Thou payest me,
Kuppaumeh.
Thou payest him,
Kuppaum.
Thou payest us,
Kuppaumimun.
Thou payest them,
Kuppaumoog.

3 sing.
He keepeth me,
Noowadchanuk.
He keepeth thee,
Koowadchanuk.
He keepeth him,
oowadchanuh.
He keepeth us,
Koowadchanukqun.
He keepeth you,
Koowadchanukoo.
He keepeth them,
oowadchanuh.

3 plut.
He payeth me,
Nuppaumuk.
He payeth thee,
Kuppaumuk.
He payeth him,
Uppaumuh.
He payeth us,
Kuppaumukqun.
He payeth you,
Kuppaumukou.
He payeth them,
Uppaumuh nah.

Indicative Mode.

Prefent tenfe.

1 *plur.*

> We keep thee,
> Koowadchanunumun.
> We keep him,
> noowadchanoun.
> We keep you,
> koowadchanunumun (wame.)
> We keep them,
> noowadchanóunonog.

2 *plur.*

> Ye keep me,
> Koowadchanimwoo.
> Ye keep him,
> koowadchanau.
> Ye keep us,
> koowadchanimun.
> Ye keep them,
> koowadchanoog.

3 *plur.*

> They keep me,
> Noowadchanukquog.
> They keep thee,
> koowadchanukquog.
> They keep him,
> oowadchanouh.
> They keep us,
> noowadchanukqunnonog.
> They keep you,
> koowadchanukoooog.
> They keep them,
> oowadchanouh nah.

Prefent tenfe.

1 *plur.*

> We pay thee,
> Kuppaumunumun.
> We pay him,
> nuppaumoun.
> We pay you,
> kuppaumunumun.
> We pay them,
> nuppaumounónog.

2 *plur.*

> Ye pay me,
> Kuppaumimwoo.
> Ye pay him,
> kuppaumau.
> Ye pay us,
> kuppaumimun.
> Ye pay them,
> kuppaumoog.

3 *plur.*

> They pay me,
> Nuppaumukquog.
> They pay thee,
> kuppaumukquog.
> They pay him,
> uppaumouh.
> They pay us,
> nuppaumukqunnonog.
> They pay you,
> kuppaumukoooog.
> They pay them,
> uppaumouh nah.

E

Indicative

Indicative Mode.

Present tense.

1 plut.
We keep thee,
Koowadchanunumun.
We keep him,
noowadchanoun.
We keep you,
koowadchanunumun (wame.)
We keep them,
noowadchanóunonog.

2 plut.
Ye keep me,
Koowadchanimwoo.
Ye keep him,
koowadchanau.
Ye keep us,
koowadchanimun.
Ye keep them,
koowadchanoog.

3 plut.
They keep me,
Noowadchanukquog.
They keep thee,
koowadchanukquog.
They keep him,
oowadchanouh.
They keep us,
noowadchanukqunnonog.
They keep you,
koowadchanukoooog.
They keep them,
oowadchanouh nah.

Present tense.

1 plur.
We pay thee,
Kuppaumunumun.
We pay him,
nuppaumoun.
We pay you,
kuppaumunumun.
We pay them,
nuppaumounónog.

2 plur.
Ye pay me,
Kuppaumimwoo.
Ye pay him,
kuppaumau.
Ye pay us,
kuppaumimun.
Ye pay them,
kuppaumoog.

3 plut.
They pay me,
Nuppaumukquog.
They pay thee,
kuppaumukquog.
They pay him,
uppaumouh.
They pay us,
nuppaumukqunnonog.
They pay you,
kuppaumukoooog.
They pay them,
uppaumouh nah.

Indicative Mode.

Præter tense.   *Præter tense.*

1 sing.
I did keep thee,
Koowadchanunup.
I did keep him,
noowadchanóp.
I did keep you,
koowadchanunnumwop.
I did keep them,
noowadchanópanneg.

1 sing.
I did pay thee,
Kuppaumunup.
I did pay him,
nuppaumóp.
I did pay you,
kuppaumunumwop.
I did pay them,
nuppaumópanneg.

2 sing.
Thou didst keep me,
Koowadchanip.
Thou didst keep him,
koowadchanóp.
Thou didst keep us,
koowadchanimunonup.
Thou didst keep them,
koowadchanopanneg.

2 sing.
Thou didst pay me,
Kuppaumip.
Thou didst pay him,
kuppaumóp.
Thou didst pay us,
kuppaumimunonup.
Thou didst pay them,
kuppaumopanneg.

3 sing.
He did keep me,
Noowadchanukup.
He did keep thee,
koowadchanukup.
He did keep him,
oowadchanópoh.
He did keep us,
noowadchanukqunnonup.
He did keep you,
koowadchanukooop.
He did keep them,
oowadchanoóópoh.

3 sing.
He did pay me,
Nuppaumukup.
He did pay thee,
kuppaumukup.
He did pay him,
uppaumopoh.
He did pay us,
nuppaumukqunnonup.
He did pay you,
kuppaumukoowop.
He did pay them,
uppaumopoh nah.

Indicative Mode.

Præter tense.

1 sing.
{
I did keep thee,
Kꝏwadchanunup.
I did keep him,
nꝏwadchanóp.
I did keep you,
kꝏwadchanunnumwop.
I did keep them,
nꝏwadchanópanneg.
}

2 sing.
{
Thou didst keep me,
Kꝏwadchanip.
Thou didst keep him,
kꝏwadchanóp.
Thou didst keep us,
kꝏwadchanimunonup.
Thou didst keep them,
kꝏwadchanopanneg.
}

3 sing.
{
He did keep me,
Nꝏwadchanukup.
He did keep thee,
kꝏwadchanukup.
He did keep him,
ꝏwadchanópoh.
He did keep us,
nꝏwadchanukqunnonup.
He did keep you,
kꝏwadchanukꝏop.
He did keep them,
ꝏwadchanꝏópoh.
}

Præter tense.

1 sing.
{
I did pay thee,
Kuppaumunup.
I did pay him,
nuppaumóp.
I did pay you,
kuppaumunumwop.
I did pay them,
nuppaumópanneg.
}

2 sing.
{
Thou didst pay me,
Kuppaumip.
Thou didst pay him,
kuppaumóp.
Thou didst pay us,
kuppaumimunonup.
Thou didst pay them,
kuppaumopanneg.
}

3 sing.
{
He did pay me,
Nuppaumukup.
He did pay thee,
kuppaumukup.
He did pay him,
uppaumopoh.
He did pay us,
nuppaumukqunnonup.
He did pay you,
kuppaumukꝏwop.
He did pay them,
uppaumopoh nah.
}

Indicative Mode.

Præter tense.

We did keep thee,
Kꝏwadchaninumunonup
We did keep him,
nꝏwadchanóunonup
We did keep you,
kꝏwadchaninumunonup
We did keep them,
nꝏwadchanounonuppanneg.

Ye did keep me,
Kꝏwadchanimwop.
Ye did keep him,
kꝏwadchanuop.
Ye did keep us,
kꝏwadchanimunonup.
Ye did keep them,
kꝏwadchanoopanneg.

They did keep me,
Nꝏwadchanukuppanneg.
They did keep thee,
kꝏwadchanukuppanneg.
They did keep him,
ꝏwadchanauopoh.
They did keep us, [neg.
kꝏwadchanukqunonuppan-
They did keep you,
kꝏwadchanukꝏoopanneg.
They did keep them,
ꝏwadchanꝏopoh nah.

Præter tense.

we did pay thee,
kuppaumunumunonup.
We did pay him,
nuppaumounonup.
We did pay you,
kuppaumunumunonup.
We did pay them,
nnppaumounonuppanneg

Ye did pay me,
Kuppaumimwop.
Ye did pay him,
kuppaumauop.
Ye did pay us,
kuppaumimunonup.
Ye did pay them,
kuppaumauopanneg.

They did pay me,
Nuppaumukuppaneg.
They did pay thee,
kuppaumukuppanneg.
They did pay him,
uppaumauopoh.
They did pay us,
nuppaumukqunnouppanneg.
They did pay you,
kuppaumukꝏopanneg.
They did pay them,
uppaumꝏopoh nah.

1 *plur.* ... 2 *plur.* ... 3 *plur.*

The

Indicative Mode.

Præter tense.

1 plur.

We did keep thee,
Kꝏwadchaninumunonup.
We did keep him,
nꝏwadchanóunonup.
We did keep you,
kꝏwadchaninumunonup.
We did keep them,
nꝏwadchanounonuppanneg.

2 plur.

Ye did keep me,
Kꝏwadchanimwop.
Ye did keep him,
kꝏwadchanuop.
Ye did keep us,
kꝏwadchanimunonup.
Ye did keep them,
kꝏwadchanoopanneg.

3 plur.

They did keep me,
Nꝏwadchanukuppanneg.
They did keep thee,
kꝏwadchanukuppanneg.
They did keep him,
ꝏwadchanauopoh.
They did keep us,
kꝏwadchanukqunonuppanneg.
They did keep you,
kꝏwadchanukꝏoopanneg.
They did keep them,
ꝏwadchanꝏopoh nah.

Præter tense.

1 plur.

We did pay thee,
kuppaumunumunonup.
We did pay him,
nuppaumounonup.
We did pay you,
kuppaumunumunonup.
We did pay them,
nuppaumounonuppanneg.

2 plur.

Ye did pay me,
Kuppaumimwop.
Ye did pay him,
kuppaumauop.
Ye did pay us,
kuppaumimunonup.
Ye did pay them,
kuppaumauopanneg.

3 plur.

They did pay me,
Nuppaumukuppaneg.
They did pay thee,
kuppaumukuppanneg.
They did pay him,
uppaumauopoh.
They did pay us,
nuppaumukqunnouppanneg.
They did pay you,
kuppaumukꝏopanneg.
They did pay them,
uppaumꝏopoh nah.

The *Imperative Mode* of the *Suffix form animate Affirmative.*

Note, That this Mode of the Verb doth caſt off the *Affix,* or *prefixed Pronoun,*
uſing onely the *ſuffixed Grammaticall variations.*

Preſent tenſe.

1 *ſing.*
- Let me keep thee, Wanchanunutti.
- Let me keep him, wadchanônti.
- Let me keep you, wadchanunonkqutch.
- Let me keep them, wadchanonti nagoh.

2 *ſing.*
- Do thou keep me, Wadchaneh.
- Do thou keep him, wadchan.
- Do thou keep us, wadchaninnean.
- Do thou keep them, wadchan nag.

3 *ſing.*
- Let him keep me, Wadchanitch.
- Let him keep thee, wadchanukquſh.
- Let him keep him, wadchanonch.
- Let him keep us, wadchanukqutteuh.
- Let him keep you, wadchanukôok.
- Let him keep them, wanchanonch.

Preſent tenſe.

1 *ſing.*
- Let me pay thee, Paumunutti.
- Let me pay him, paumonti.
- Let me pay you, paumunonkqutch.
- Let me pay them, paumonti.

2 *ſing.*
- Do thou pay me, Paumeh.
- Do thou pay him, paum.
- Do thou pay us, pauminnean.
- Do thou pay them, paum.

3 *ſing.*
- Let him pay me, Paumitch.
- Let him pay thee, paumukquſh.
- Let him pay him, paumonch.
- Let him pay us, paumukqutteuh.
- Let him pay you, paumukôok.
- Let him pay them, paumonch.

Imperative

The *Imperative Mode* of the *Suffix form animate Affirmative.*

Note, That this Mode of the Verb doth cast off the *Affix,* or *prefixed Pronoun,* using onely the suffixed *Grammaticall variations.*

1 sing.

Present tense.
Let me keep thee,
Wanchanunutti.
Let me keep him,
wadchanonti.
Let me keep you,
wadchanunonkqutch.
Let me keep them,
wadchanonti nagoh.

Present tense.
Let me pay thee,
Paumunutti.
Let me pay him,
paumonti.
Let me pay you,
paumunonkqutch.
Let me pay them,
paumonti.

2 sing.

Do thou keep me,
Wadchaneh.
Do thou keep him,
wadchan.
Do thou keep us,
wadchaninnean.
Do thou keep them,
wadchan nag.

Do thou pay me,
Paumeh.
Do thou pay him,
paum.
Do thou pay us,
pauminnean.
Do thou pay them,
paum.

3 sing.

Let him keep me,
Wadchanitch.
Let him keep thee,
wadchanukqush.
Let him keep him,
wadchanonch.
Let him keep us,
wadchanukqutteuh.
Let him keep you,
wadchanukook.
Let him keep them,
wanchanonch.

Let him pay me,
Paumitch.
Let him pay thee,
paumukqush.
Let him pay him,
paumonch.
Let him pay us,
paumukqutteuh.
Let him pay you,
paumukook.
Let him pay them,
paumonch.

Imperative Mode.

Prefent tenfe.

Let us keep thee,
Wadchanunuttuh.
Let us keep him,
wadchanontuh.
Let us keep you,
wadchanunuttuh.
Let us keep them,
wadchanontuh.

(1 plur.)

Let us pay thee,
Paumunuttuh.
Let us pay him,
paumontuh.
Let us pay you,
paumunuttuh.
Let us pay them,
paumontuh.

(1 plur.)

Do ye keep me,
Wadchanegk.
Do ye keep him,
wadchanók.
De ye keep us,
wadchaninnean.
Let us keep them,
wadchanók.

(2 plur.)

Do ye pay me,
Paumegk.
Do ye pay him,
paumók.
Do ye pay us,
pauminnean.
Do ye pay them.
paumók.

(2 plur.)

Let them keep me,
Wadchanukquttei, *or* wad-
     chanhettich.
Let them keep thee,
wadchanukquſh.
Let them keep him,
wadchanáhettich.
Let them keep us,
wadchanukqutteuh.
Let them keep you,
wadchanukook.
Let them keep them,
wadchanáhettich.

(3 plur.)

Let them pay me,
Paumukquttei, *or* Paumé-
     hettich.
Let them pay thee,
paumukquſh.
Let them pay him,
paumáhettich.
Let them pay us,
paumukqutteuh.
Let them pay you,
paumukook.
Let them pay them,
paumáhettich.

(3 plur.)

The

Imperative Mode.

Present tense.

1 plur. {
Let us keep thee,
Wadchanunuttuh.
Let us keep him,
wadchanontuh.
Let us keep you,
wadchanunuttuh.
Let us keep them,
wadchanontuh.
}

2 plur. {
Do ye keep me,
Wadchanegk.
Do ye keep him,
wadchanók.
Do ye keep us,
wadchaninnean.
Do ye keep them,
wadchanók.
}

3 plur. {
Let them keep me,
Wadchanukquttei, *or* wad-
   chanhettich
Let them keep thee,
wadchanukqush.
Let them keep him,
wadchanáhettich.
Let them keep us,
wadchanukqutteuh.
Let them keep you,
wadchanukꝏk.
Let them keep them,
wanchanáhettich.
}

Present tense.

1 plur. {
Let us pay thee,
Paumunuttuh.
Let us pay him,
paumontuh.
Let us pay you,
paumunuttuh.
Let us pay them,
paumontuh.
}

2 plur. {
Do ye pay me,
Paumegk.
Do ye pay him,
paumók.
Do ye pay us,
pauminnean.
Do ye pay them,
paumók.
}

3 plur. {
Let them pay me,
Paumukquttei, *or* Paumé-
   hettich.
Let them pay thee,
paumukqush.
Let them pay him,
paumáhettich.
Let them pay us,
paumukqutteuh.
Let them pay you,
paumukꝏk.
Let them pay them,
paumáhettich.
}

The *Optative Mode* of the *Suffix form animate Affirmative.*

This *Adverb* (toh) *or* (napehnonr) ;*properly* fignifieth (utinam) *I wifh it were.*
And fee how naturally they annex it unto every variation of this Mode of the
Verb. Note alfo, That this Mode keepeth the Affix, or prefixed Pro-
noun.

Prefent tenfe.

1 fing.
- I Wifh I keep thee, [pehnont Koowaadchanunan-toh, *or* na-
- I wifh I keep him, Noowaadchanun-toh.
- I wifh I keep you, Koowaadchanununeau-toh.
- I wifh I keep them, Noowaadchanóneau-toh.

2 fing.
- I wifh thou keep me, Koowaadchanin-toh.
- I wifh thou keep him, koowaadchanon-toh.
- I Wifh thou keep us, koowaadchaninneau-toh.
- I Wifh thou keep them, koowaadchanoneauh-toh.

3 fing.
- I Wifh he keepe me, Noowaadchanukqun-toh.
- I wifh he keep thee, koowaadchanukqun-toh.
- I wifh he keep him, oowaadchanon-toh.
- I wifh he keep us, koowaadchanukqunan-toh.
- I wifh he keep you, koowaadchanukquneau-toh.
- I wifh he keep them, oowaadchanon-toh.

Prefent tenfe.

1 fing.
- I Wifh I pay thee, Kuppapaumunun-toh.
- I wifh I pay him, nuppapaumon-toh.
- I wifh I pay you, kuppapaumuneau-toh.
- I Wifh I pay them, nuppapaumóneau-toh.

2 fing.
- I Wifh thou pay me, kuppapaumin-toh.
- I wifh thou pay him, kuppapaumon-toh.
- I wifh thou pay us, kuppapaumuneau-toh.
- I wifh thou pay them, kuppapaumóneau-toh.

3 fing.
- I Wifh he pay me, Nuppapaumukqun-toh.
- I wifh he pay thee, kuppapaumukqun-toh.
- I wifh he pay him, uppapaumon-toh.
- I wifh he pay us, kuppapaumukqunan-toh.
- I wifh he pay you, kuppapaumukquneau-toh.
- I wifh he pay them, uppapaumon-toh.

Optative

The *Optative Mode* of the *Suffix form animate Affirmative.*

This Adverb (toh) *or* (napehnont) *; properly signifieth* (utinam) *I wish it were.*
And see how naturally they annex it unto every variation of this Mode of
the Verb. Note also, That this Mode keepeth the Affix, or prefixed
Pronoun.

Present tense.

1 sing.
{ *I wish I keep thee,* [pehnont
Koowaadchanunan-toh, *or* na-
I wish I keep him,
Noowaadchanun-toh.
I wish I keep you,
Koowaadchanununeau-toh.
I wish I keep them,
Noowaadchanóneau-toh. }

Present tense.

1 sing.
{ *I wish I pay thee,*
Kuppapaumunun-toh.
I wish I pay him,
nuppapaumon-toh.
I wish I pay you,
kuppapaumuneau-toh.
I wish I pay them,
nuppapaumóneau-toh. }

2 sing.
{ *I wish thou keep me,*
Koowaadchanin-toh.
I wish thou keep him,
koowaadchanon-toh.
I wish thou keep us,
koowaadchaninneau-toh.
I wish thou keep them,
koowaadchanoneauh-toh. }

2 sing.
{ *I wish thou pay me,*
kuppapaumin-toh.
I wish thou pay him,
kuppapaumon-toh.
I wish thou pay us,
kuppapaumuneau-toh.
I wish thou pay them,
kuppapaumóneau-toh. }

3 sing.
{ *I wish he keep me,*
Noowaadchanukqun-toh.
I wish he keep thee,
koowaadchanukqun-toh.
I wish he keep him,
oowaadchanon-toh.
I wish he keep us,
koowaadchanukqunan-toh.
I wish he keep you,
koowaadchanukquneau-toh.
I wish he keep them,
oowaadchanon-toh. }

3 sing.
{ *I wish he pay me,*
Nuppapaumukqun-toh.
I wish he pay thee,
kuppapaumukqun-toh.
I wish he pay him,
uppapaumon-toh.
I wish he pay us,
kuppapaumukqunan-toh.
I wish he pay you,
kuppapaumukquneau-toh.
I wish he pay them,
uppapaumon-toh. }

Optative Mode.

Prefent tenfe.

1 plur.
- *I wish we keep thee,*
  Koowaadchanunan-toh.
- *I wish we keep him,*
  noowaadchanonan-toh.
- *I wish we keep you,*
  koowaadchanunnan-toh.
- *I wish we keep them,*
  noowaadchanonan-toh.

2 plur.
- *I wish ye keep me,*
  Koowaadchanuneau-toh.
- *I wish ye keep him,*
  koowaadchanóneau-toh.
- *I wish ye keep us,*
  koowaadchanunean-toh.
- *I wish ye keep them,*
  koowaadchanóneau-toh.

3 plur.
- *I wish they keep me,*
  Noowaadchanukquneau-toh.
- *I wish they keep thee,*
  koowaadchanukquneau-toh.
- *I wish they keep him,*
  oowaadchanoneau-toh.
- *I wish they keep us,*
  noowaadchanukqunan-toh.
- *I wish they keep you,*
  koowaadchanukquneau-toh.
- *I wish they keep them,*
  oowaadchanoneau-toh.

Prefent tenfe.

1 plur.
- *I wish we pay thee.*
  Kuppapaumunan-toh.
- *I wish we pay him,*
  nuppapaumónan-toh.
- *I wish we pay you,*
  kuppapaumunan-toh.
- *I wish we pay them,*
  nuppapaumonan-toh.

2 plur.
- *I wish ye pay me,*
  Kuppapaumuneau-toh.
- *I wish ye pay him,*
  kuppapaumóneau-toh.
- *I wish ye pay us,*
  kuppapaumunean-toh.
- *I wish ye pay them,*
  kuppapaumóneau-toh.

3 plur.
- *I wish they pay me,*
  Nuppapaumukquneau-toh.
- *I wish they pay thee,*
  kuppapaumukquneau-toh.
- *I wish they him,*
  uppapaumóneau-toh.
- *I wish they pay us,*
  nuppapaumukqunan-toh.
- *I wish they pay you,*
  kuppapaumukquneau-toh.
- *I wish they pay them,*
  uppapaumóneau-toh.

Optative

Optative Mode.

Present tense. *Present tense.*

1 plur.
{
I wish we keep thee,
Kꝏwaadchanunan-toh.
I wish we keep him,
nꝏwaadchanonan-toh.
I wish we keep you,
kꝏwaadchanunnan-toh.
I wish we keep them,
nꝏwaadchanonan-toh.
}

1 plur.
{
I wish we pay thee,
Kuppapaumunan-toh.
I wish we pay him,
nuppapaumónan-toh.
I wish we pay you,
kuppapaumunan-toh.
I wish we pay them,
nuppapaumonan-toh.
}

2 plur.
{
I wish ye keep me,
Kꝏwaadchanuneau-toh.
I wish ye keep him,
kꝏwaadchanóneau-toh.
I wish ye keep us,
kꝏwaadchanunean-toh.
I wish ye keep them,
kꝏwaadchanóneau-toh.
}

2 plur.
{
I wish ye pay me,
Kuppapaumuneau-toh.
I wish ye pay him,
kuppapaumóneau-toh.
I wish ye pay us,
kuppapaumunean-toh.
I wish ye pay them,
kuppapaumoneau-toh.
}

3 plur.
{
I wish they keep me,
Nꝏwaadchanukquneau-toh.
I wish they keep thee,
kꝏwaadchanukquneau-toh.
I wish they keep him,
ꝏwaadchanoneau-toh.
I wish they keep us,
nꝏwaadchanukqunan-toh.
I wish they keep you,
kꝏwaadchanukquneau-toh.
I wish they keep them,
ꝏwaadchanoneau-toh.
}

3 plur.
{
I wish they pay me,
Nuppapaumukquneau-toh.
I wish they pay thee,
kuppapaumukquneau-toh.
I wish they pay him,
uppapaumóneau-toh.
I wish they pay us,
nuppapaumukqunan-toh.
I wish they pay you,
kuppapaumukquneau-toh.
I wish they pay them,
uppapaumóneau-toh.
}

Optative Mode.

Præter tense.   *Præter tense.*

1 sing.

I wish I did keep thee,
Koowaadchanununaz-toh.
I wish I did keep him,
noowaadchanónaz-toh.
I wish I did keep you,
koowaadchanununnaouz-toh.
I wish I did keep them,
noowaadchanónaóoz-toh.

I wish I did pay thee,
Kuppapaumununaz-toh.
I wish I did pay him,
nuppapaumónaz-toh.
I wish I did pay you,
kuppapaumununnaouz-toh.
I wish I did pay them,
nuppapaumonaouz-toh.

2 sing.

I wish thou didst keep me,
Koowaadchaninneaz-toh.
I wish thou didst keep him,
koowaadchanónaz-toh.
I wish thou didst keep us,
koowaadchanuneanonuz-toh
I wish thou didst keep them,
koowaadchanónaouz-toh.

I wish thou didst pay me,
Kuppapaumineaz-toh.
I wish thou didst pay him,
kuppapaumonaz-toh.
I wish thou didst pay us,
kuppapaumuneanonuz-toh.
I wish thou didst pay them,
kuppapaumónaouz-toh.

3 sing.

I wish he did keep me,
Noowadchanukqunaz-toh.
I wish he did keep thee,
koowaadchanukqunaz-toh.
I wish he did keep him,
oowaadchanónaz-toh.
I wish he did keep us,
noowaadchanukqunanonuz-toh
I wish he did keep you,
koowaadchanukqunnaouz-toh.
I wish he did keep them,
oowaadchanonaouz-toh.

I wish he did pay me,
Nuppapaumukqunaz-toh.
I wish he did pay thee,
kuppapaumukqunaz-toh.
I wish he did pay him,
uppapaumónaz-toh.
I wish he did pay us,
nuppapaumukqunanonuz-toh
I wish he did pay you,
kuppapaumukqunaouz-toh.
I wish he did pay them,
uppapaumonaouz-toh.

Optative

Optative Mode.

Præter tense.

1 sing.

{
I wish I did keep thee,
Kꝏwaadchanununaz-toh.
I wish I did keep him,
nꝏwaadchanónaz-toh.
I wish I did keep you,
kꝏwaadchanununnaouz-toh.
I wish I did keep them,
nꝏwaadchanónaóoz-toh.
}

1 sing.

{
I wish I did pay thee,
Kuppapaumununaz-toh.
I wish I did pay him,
nuppapaumónaz-toh.
I wish I did pay you,
kuppapaumununnaouz-toh.
I wish I did pay them,
nuppapaumonaouz-toh.
}

2 sing.

{
I wish thou didst keep me,
Kꝏwaadchaninneaz-toh.
I wish thou didst keep him,
kꝏwaadchanónaz-toh.
I wish thou didst keep us,
kꝏwaadchanuneanonuz-toh.
I wish thou didst keep them,
kꝏwaadchanónaouz-toh.
}

2 sing.

{
I wish thou didst pay me,
Kuppapaumineaz-toh.
I wish thou didst pay him,
kuppapaumonaz-toh.
I wish thou didst pay us,
kuppapaumuneanonuz-toh.
I wish thou didst pay them,
kuppapaumónaouz-toh.
}

3 sing.

{
I wish he did keep me,
Nꝏwadchanukqunaz-toh.
I wish he did keep thee,
kꝏwaadchanukqunaz-toh.
I wish he did keep him,
ꝏwaadchanónaz-toh.
I wish he did keep us,
nꝏwaadchanukqunanonuz-toh.
I wish he did keep you,
kꝏwaadchanukqunnaouz-toh.
I wish he did keep them,
ꝏwaadchanonaouz-toh.
}

3 sing.

{
I wish he did pay me,
Nuppapaumukqunaz-toh.
I wish he did pay thee,
kuppapaumukqunaz-toh.
I wish he did pay him,
uppapaumónaz-toh.
I wish he did pay us,
nuppapaumukqunanonuz-toh.
I wish he did pay you,
kuppapaumukqunaouz-toh.
I wish he did pay them,
uppapaumonaouz-toh.
}

Optative Mode.

Prater tenfe.

1 plur.
- I wish we did keep thee,
  Koowaadchanonanonuz-toh.
- I wish we did keep him,
  noowaadchanonanonuz-toh.
- I Wish we did keep you,
  koowaadchanunanonaz-toh.
- I wish we did keep them,
  noowaadchanonanonuz-toh.

2 plur.
- I wish ye did keep me,
  Koowaadchanineaouz-toh.
- I Wish ye did keep him,
  koowaadchanonaouz-toh.
- I wish ye did keep us,
  koowaadchaninneanonuz-toh.
- I Wish ye did keep them,
  koowaadchanonaouz-toh.

3 plur.
- I wish they did keep me,
  Noowaadchanukqunnaouz-toh.
- I wish they did keep thee,
  koowaadchanukqunaouz-toh.
- I Wish they did keep him,
  oowaadchanonaouz—toh.
- I wish they did keep us,
  noowaadchanukqunnanouz-toh.
- I wish they did keep you,
  koowaadchanukqunaouz-toh.
- I wish they did keep them,
  oowaadchanonaouz-toh.

Prater tenfe.

1 plur.
- I wish we did pay thee,
  Kuppapaumunanonuz-toh.
- I wish we did pay him,
  nuppapaumonanonuz-toh.
- I wish we did pay you,
  kuppapaumunanonuz-toh.
- I Wish we did pay them,
  nuppapaumonanonuz-toh.

2 plur.
- I wish ye did pay me,
  Kuppapaumineaouz-toh.
- I wish ye did pay him,
  kuppapaumonaouz-toh.
- I wish ye did pay us,
  kuppapaumineanonuz-toh.
- I wish ye did pay them,
  kuppapaumonaouz-toh.

3 plur.
- I wish they did pay me,
  Nuppapaumukqunaouz-toh.
- I wish they did pay thee,
  kuppapaumukqunaouz-toh.
- I wish they did pay him,
  uppapaumonaouz-toh.
- I wish they did pay us,
  nuppapaumukqunanonuz-toh
- I wish they did pay you,
  kuppapaumukqunaouz—toh.
- I wish they did pay them,
  uppapaumonaouz-toh.

The

Optative Mode.

Præter tense.

1 plur.
I wish we did keep thee,
Koowaadchanònanonuz-toh.
I wish we did keep him,
noowaadchanònanonuz-toh.
I wish we did keep you,
koowaadchanunanònaz-toh.
I wish we did keep them,
noowaadchanonanonuz-toh.

2 plur.
I wish ye did keep me,
Koowaadchanineaouz-toh.
I wish ye did keep him,
koowaadchanonaóuz-toh.
I wish ye did keep us,
koowaadchaninneanonuz-toh.
I wish ye did keep them,
koowaadchanónaouz-toh.

3 plur.
I wish they did keep me,
Noowaadchanukqunnaz-toh.
I wish they did keep thee,
koowaadchanukqunaóuz-toh.
I wish they did keep him,
oowaadchanonaóuz-toh.
I wish they did keep us,
noowaadchanukqunnanonuz-toh.
I wish they did keep you,
koowaadchanukqunaóuz-toh.
I wish they did keep them,
oowaadchanónaouz-toh.

Præter tense.

1 plur.
I wish we did pay thee,
Kuppapaumunanonuz-toh.
I wish we did pay him,
nuppapaumónanonuz-toh.
I wish we did pay you,
kuppapaumunanonuz-toh.
I wish we did pay them,
nuppapaumonanonuz-toh.

2 plur.
I wish ye did pay me,
Kuppapaumineaouz-toh.
I wish ye did pay him,
kuppapaumonaouz-toh.
I wish ye did pay us,
kuppapaumineanonuz-toh.
I wish thou did pay them,
kuppapaumonaouz-toh.

3 plur.
I wish they did pay me,
Nuppapaumukqunaouz-toh.
I wish they did pay thee,
kuppapaumukqunaóuz-toh.
I wish they did pay him,
uppapaumónaòuz-toh.
I wish they did pay us,
nuppapaumukqunanonuz-toh.
I wish they did pay you,
kuppapaumukqunaòuz-toh.
I wish they did pay them,
uppapaumónaouz-toh.

The *Suppofitive Mode* of the *Suffix form animate Affirmative.*

Note, That this Mode alfo doth caft off the Affix, or prefixed Pronoun.

Prefent tenfe.	*Prefent tenfe.*

1 *fing.*
- *If I keep thee,* Wadchanunon.
- *If I keep him,* wadchanog.
- *If I keep you,* wadchanunog.
- *If I keep them,* wadchaog.

1. *fing.*
- *If I pay thee,* Paumunon.
- *If I pay him,* paumog.
- *If I pay you,* paumunóg.
- *If I pay them,* paumog.

2 *fing.*
- *If thou keep me,* Wadchanean.
- *If thou keep him,* wadchanadt.
- *If thou keep us,* wadchaneog.
- *If thou keep them,* wadchanadt.

2 *fing.*
- *If thou pay me,* Paumean.
- *If thou pay him,* paumadt.
- *If thou pay us,* paumeog.
- *If thou pay them,* paumadt.

3 *fing.*
- *If he keep me,* Wadchanit.
- *If he keep thee,* wadchanukquean.
- *If he keep him,* wadchanont.
- *If he keep us,* wadchanukqueog.
- *If he keep you,* wadchanukqueóg.
- *If he keep them,* wadchanáhettit, *or* ont.

3 *fing.*
- *If he pay me,* Paumit.
- *If he pay thee,* paumukquean.
- *If he pay him,* paumont.
- *If he pay us,* paumukqueog.
- *If he pay you,* paumukqueog.
- *If he pay them,* paumáhettit.

Suppofitive

The *Suppositive Mode* of the *Suffix form animate Affirmative.*

Note, That this Mode also doth cast off the Affix, or prefixed Pronoun.

Present tense.
1 sing. {
If I keep thee, Wadchanunon.
If I keep him, wadchanog.
If I keep you, wadchanunog.
If I keep them, wadchaog.
}

Present tense.
1 sing. {
If I pay thee, Paumunon.
If I pay him, paumog.
If I pay you, paumunóg.
If I pay them, paumog.
}

2 sing. {
If thou keep me, Wadchanean.
If thou keep him, wadchanadt.
If thou keep us, wadchaneog.
If thou keep them, wadchanadt.
}

2 sing. {
If thou pay me, Paumean.
If thou pay him, paumadt.
If thou pay us, paumeog.
If thou pay them, paumadt.
}

3 sing. {
If he keep me, Wadchanit.
If he keep thee, wadchanukquean.
If he keep him, wadchanont.
If he keep us, wadchanukqueog.
If he keep you, wadchanukqueóg.
If he keep them, wadchanáhettit, *or* ont.
}

3 sing. {
If he pay me, Paumit.
If he pay thee, paumukquean.
If he pay him, paumont.
If he pay us, paumukqueog.
If he pay you, paumukqueog.
If he pay them, paumáhettit.
}

Suppofitive Mode.

Note, *where the fingular and plural are alike, they are diftinguifhed by* Noh *or* Neen *in the fingular, and* Nag *or* Nenawun *in the plural.*

Pr efent tenfe.

1 plur.
- If we keep thee
Wadchanunog.
- If we keep him,
wadchanogkut.
- If we keep you,
wadchanunog.
- If We keep them,
wadchanogkut.

2 plur.
- If ye keep me,
Wadchaneog.
- If ye keep him,
wadchanog.
- If ye keep us,
wadchaneog.
- If ye keep them,
wadchanog.

3 plur.
- If they keep me,
Wadchanhettit.
- If they keep thee,
wadchanukquean.
- If they keep him,
wadchanukáhettit.
- If they keep us,
wadchanukqueog.
- If they keep you,
wadchanukqueog.
- If they keep them,
wadchanáhettit.

Prefent tenfe.

1 plur.
- If we pay thee,
Paumunog.
- If we pay him,
paumogkut.
- If we pay you,
paumunog.
- If we pay them,
paumogkut.

2 plur.
- If ye pay me,
Paumeóg.
- If ye pay him,
paumóg.
- If ye pay us,
paumeóg.
- If ye pay them,
paumóg.

3 plur.
- if they pay me,
Paumhettit.
- If they pay thee,
paumukquean.
- If they pay him,
paumáhettit.
- if they pay us,
paumukqueog.
- if they pay you,
paumukqueóg.
- If they pay them.
paumáhettit.

F 2

Suppofitive

Suppositive Mode.

Note, *where the singular and plural are alike, they are distinguished by* Noh *or* Neen *in the singular, and* Nag *or* Nenawun *in the plural.*

1 plur. {
Present tense.
If we keep thee,
Wadchanunog.
If we keep him,
wadchanogkut.
If we keep you,
wadchanunog.
If we keep them,
wadchanogkut.
}

1 plur. {
Present tense.
If we pay thee,
Paumunog.
If we pay him,
paumogkut.
If we pay you,
paumunog.
If we pay them,
paumogkut.
}

2 plur. {
If ye keep me,
Wadchaneog.
If ye keep him,
wadchanog.
If ye keep us,
wadchaneog.
If ye keep them,
wadchanóg.
}

2 plur. {
If ye pay me,
Paumeóg.
If ye pay him,
paumóg.
If ye pay us,
paumeóg.
If ye pay them,
paumóg.
}

3 plur. {
If they keep me,
Wadchanhettit.
If they keep thee,
wadchanukquean.
If they keep him,
wadchanukáhettit.
If they keep us,
wadchanukqueog.
If they keep you,
wadchanukqueòg.
If they keep them,
wadchanáhettit.
}

3 plur. {
If they pay me,
Paumhettit.
If they pay thee,
paumukquean.
If they pay him,
paumáhettit.
If they pay us,
paumukqueog.
If they pay you,
paumukqueòg.
If they pay them,
paumáhettit.
}

Suppositive Mode.

Præter tenſe.   *Præter tenſe.*

1 ſing.
- If *I did keep thee,*
  Wadchanunos.
- If *I did keep him,*
  waadchanogkus.
- If *I did keep you,*
  wadchanunógkus.
- If *I did keep them,*
  wadchanogkus.

1 ſing.
- If *I did pay thee,*
  Paumunos.
- If *I did pay him,*
  paumogkus.
- If *I did pay you,*
  paumunógkus.
- If *I did pay them,*
  paumogkus.

2 ſing.
- If *thou didſt keep me,*
  Wadchaneas.
- If *thou didſt keep him,*
  wadchanas,
- If *thou didſt keep us,*
  wadchaneogkus.
- If *thou didſt keep them,*
  wadchanas.

2 ſing.
- if *thou didſt pay me,*
  Paumeas.
- If *thou didſt pay him,*
  paumas.
- If *thou didſt pay us,*
  paumeogkus.
- If *thou didſt pay them,*
  paumas.

3 ſing.
- If *he did keep me,*
  Wadchanis.
- If *he did keep thee,*
  wadchanukqueas.
- If *he did keep him,*
  wadchanós.
- If *he did keep us,*
  wadchanukqueogkus.
- If *he did keep you,*
  wadchanukqueógkus.
- If *he did keep them,*
  wadchanos.

3 ſing.
- if *he did pay me,*
  Paumis.
- If *he did pay thee,*
  paumukqueas.
- If *he did pay him,*
  paumos.
- If *he did pay us,*
  paumukqueogkus.
- If *he did pay you,*
  paumukqueogkus.
- If *he did pay them,*
  paumos.

Suppoſitive

Suppositive Mode.

Præter tense.   *Præter tense.*

1 sing.
{
If I did keep thee,
Wadchanunos.
If I did keep him,
waadchanogkus.
If I did keep you,
wadchanunógkus.
If I did keep them,
wadchanogkus.
}

1 sing.
{
If I did pay thee,
Paumunos.
If I did pay him,
paumogkus.
If I did pay you,
paumunógkus.
If I did pay them,
paumogkus.
}

2 sing.
{
If thou didst keep me,
Wadchaneas.
If thou didst keep him,
wadchanas.
If thou didst keep us,
wadchaneogkus.
If thou didst keep them,
wadchanas.
}

2 sing.
{
If thou didst pay me,
Paumeas.
If thou didst pay him,
paumas.
If thou didst pay us,
paumeogkus.
If thou didst pay them,
paumas.
}

3 sing.
{
If he did keep me,
Wadchanis.
If he did keep thee,
wadchanukqueas.
If he did keep him,
wadchanós.
If he did keep us,
wadchanukqueogkus.
If he did keep you,
wadchanukqueógkus.
If he did keep them,
wadchanos.
}

3 sing.
{
If he did pay me,
Paumis.
If he did pay thee,
paumukqueas.
If he did pay him,
paumos.
If he did pay us,
paumukqueogkus.
If he did pay you,
paumukqueogkus.
If he did pay them,
paumos.
}

Suppofitive Mode.

Præter tenfe.

1 plur.
- *If we did keep thee,* Wadchanunogkus.
- *If we did keep him,* wadchanogkutus.
- *If we did keep you,* wadchanunogkus.
- *If we did keep them,* wadchanogkutus.

2 plur.
- *If ye did keep me,* Wadchaneógkus.
- *If ye did keep him,* wadchanógkus.
- *If ye did keep us,* wadchaneogkus.
- *If ye did keep them,* wadchanógkus.

3 plur.
- *If they did keep me,* Wadchanhettis.
- *If they did keep thee,* wadchanukqueas.
- *If they did keep him,* wadchanahettis.
- *If they did keep us,* wadchanukqueogkus.
- *If they keep you,* wadchanukqueógkus.
- *If they did keep them,* wadchanahettis.

Præter tenfe.

1 plur.
- *If we did pay thee,* Paumunogkus
- *If we did pay him,* paumunogkutus.
- *If we did pay you,* paumunogkus.
- *If we did pay them,* paumogkutus.

2 plur.
- *If ye did pay me,* Paumeogkus.
- *If ye did pay him,* paumogkus.
- *If ye did pay us,* paumeogkus.
- *If ye did pay them,* paumógkus.

3 plur.
- *If they did pay me,* Paumehettis.
- *If they did pay thee,* paumukqueas.
- *If they did pay him,* paumahettis.
- *If they did pay us,* paumukqueogkus.
- *If they did pay you,* paumukqueógkus.
- *If they did pay them,* paumahettis.

The

Suppositive Mode.

Præter tense.   *Præter tense.*

1 *plur.* {
If we did keep thee,
Wadchanunogkus.
If we did keep him,
wadchanogkutus.
If we did keep you,
wadchanunogkus.
If we did keep them,
wadchanogkutus.
}

1 *plur.* {
If we did pay thee,
Paumunogkus.
If we did pay him,
paumunogkutus.
If we did pay you,
paumunogkus.
If we did pay them,
paumogkutus.
}

2 *plur.* {
If ye did keep me,
Wadchaneógkus.
If ye did keep him,
wadchanógkus.
If ye did keep us,
wadchaneogkus.
If ye did keep them,
wadchanógkus.
}

2 *plur.* {
If ye did pay me,
Paumeogkus.
If ye did pay him,
paumogkus.
If ye did pay us,
paumeogkus.
If ye did pay them,
paumógkus.
}

3 *plur.* {
If they did keep me,
Wadchanhettis.
If they did keep thee,
wadchanukqueas.
If they did keep him,
wadchanahettis.
If they did keep us,
wadchanukqueogkus.
If they did keep you,
wadchanukqueógkus.
If they did keep them,
wadchanahettis.
}

3 *plur.* {
If they did pay me,
Paumehettis.
If they did pay thee,
paumukqueas.
If they did pay him,
paumahettis.
If they did pay us,
paumukqueogkus.
If they did pay you,
paumukqueógkus.
If they did pay them,
paumahettis.
}

The Indefinite Mode.

Present tense.   *Present tense.*

To keep,   *To pay,*
Wadchanónat   Paummuonat.

The *third* Person of the *Suffix form Animate* is capable to be expreſſed in the *Indefinite Mode.*

Note alſo, *That this Mode followeth the* Indicative, *and keepeth the Affix.*

As for Example.

To keep me, Noowadchanukqunat.	*To pay me,* Nuppaumunkqunat.
To keep thee, koowadchanukqunat.	*To pay thee,* kuppaumukqunat.
To keep him: oowadchanonat.	*To pay him,* uppaumonat.
To keep us, noowadchanukqunnanonut.	*To pay us,* nuppaumukqunnanonut.
To keep you. koowadchanukqunnaout.	*To pay you,* kuppaumukqunnaout.
To keep them, oowadchanónaout.	*To pay them,* uppaumonaoont.

3 *sing.* (left group)   3 *sing.* (right group)

So much for the Suffix form Animate Affirmative.

The Indefinite Mode.

Present tense.   *Present tense.*

To keep,   *To pay,*
Wadchanónat.   Paummuonat.

The *third Person* of the *Suffix form Animate* is capable to be expressed in the *Indefinite Mode.*

Note also, *That this Mode followeth the* Indicative, *and keepeth the Affix.*

As for Example.

3 sing.
{
To keep me,
Noowadchanukqunat.
To keep thee,
koowadchanukqunat.
To keep him,
oowadchanonat.
To keep us,
noowadchanukqunnanonut.
To keep you,
koowadchanukqunnaout.
To keep them,
oowadchanonaout.
}

3 sing.
{
To pay me,
Nuppaumunkqunat.
To pay thee,
kuppaumukqunat.
To pay him,
uppaumonat.
To pay us,
nuppaumukqunnanonut.
To pay you,
kuppaumukqunnaout.
To pay them,
uppaumonaoont.
}

So much for the Suffix form Animate **Affirmative.**

Page 43 was blank in the original edition,

43　*The* Indian *Grammar begun.*

Page 43 was blank in the original edition,

The *Suffix form Animate* Negative.

Indicative Mode.

Present tense.

I keep not thee,
Koowadchanunooh.
I keep not him,
noowadchanôh.
I keep not you,
koowadchanoog.
I keep not them,
Mat noowadchanoog.

Thou keep not me,
Koowadchaneúh.
Thou keep not him,
koowadchanôh.
Thou keep not us,
koowadchaneumun.
Thou keep not them,
Mat koowadchanoog.

He keep not me,
Noowadchanukooh.
He keep not thee,
koowadchanukooh.
He keep not him,
Mat oowadchanuh.
He keep not us,
noowadchanukooun.
He keep not you,
Mat koowadchanukoo.
He keep not them,
Mat oowadchanuh.

Present tense.

I pay not thee,
Kuppaumunooh.
I pay not him,
nuppaumôh.
I pay not you,
kuppaumunoomwoo.
I pay not them,
Mat nuppaumoog.

Thou pay not me,
Kuppaumeuh.
Thou pay not him,
kuppaumôh.
Thou pay not us,
kuppaumeumun.
Thou pay not them,
Mat kuppaumeumoog.

He pay not me,
Nuppaumukooh.
He pay not thee,
kuppaumukooh.
He pay not him,
Mat uppaumoh.
He pay not us,
nuppaumukooun.
He pay not you,
Mat kuppaumukooh.
He pay not them,
Mat uppaumuh.

Indicative

The *Suffix form Animate* Negative.

Indicative Mode.

Present tense.

1 sing.
I keep not thee,
Koowadchanunooh.
I keep not him,
noowadchanòh.
I keep not you,
koowadchanooh.
I keep not them,
Mat noowadchanoog.

2 sing.
Thou keep not me,
Koowadchaneúh.
Thou keep not him,
koowadchanòh.
Thou keep not us,
koowadchaneumun.
Thou keep not them,
Mat koowadchanoog.

3 sing.
He keep not me,
Noowadchanukooh.
He keep not thee,
koowadchanukooh.
He keep not him,
Mat oowadchanuh.
He keep not us,
noowadchanukooun.
He keep not you,
Mat koowadchanukoo.
He keep not them,
Mat oowadchanuh.

Present tense.

1 sing.
I pay not thee,
Kuppaumunooh.
I pay not him,
nuppaumòh.
I pay not you,
kuppaumunoomwoo.
I pay not them,
Mat nuppaumoog.

2 sing.
Thou pay not me,
Kuppaumeuh.
Thou pay not him,
kuppaumòh.
Thou pay not us,
kuppaumeumun.
Thou pay not them,
Mat kuppaumeumoog.

3 sing.
He pay not me,
Nuppaumukooh.
He pay not thee,
kuppaumukooh.
He pay not him,
Mat uppaumoh.
He pay not us,
nuppaumukooun.
He pay not you,
Mat kuppaumukooh.
He pay not them,
Mat uppaumuh.

Indicative Mode.

Prefent tenfe.

We keep not thee,
Koowadchanunoomun.
We keep not him,
mat noowadchanóun.
We keep not you,
koowadchanunoomun.
We keep not them,
mat noowadchanounonog.

1 *plur.*

Ye keep not me,
Koowadchaneumwoo.
Ye keep not him,
mat koowadchanau.
Ye keep not us,
koowadchaneumun.
Ye keep not them,
mat koowadchanoog.

2 *plur.*

They keep not me,
Noowadchanukooog.
They keep not thee,
koowadchanukooog.
They keep not him,
mat oowadchanouh.
They keep not us,
noowadchanukoounonog.
They keep not you,
koowadchanukoooog.
They keep not them,
mat oowadchanouh.

3 *plur.*

Prefent tenfe.

We pay not thee,
Kuppaumunoomun.
We pay not him,
mat nuppaumoun.
We pay not you,
kuppaumunoomun.
We pay not them,
mat nuppaumounonog.

1 *plur.*

Ye pay not me,
Kuppaumeumwoo.
Ye pay not him,
mat kuppaumau.
Ye pay not us,
kuppaumeumun.
Ye pay not them,
mat kuppaumoog.

2 *plur.*

They pay not me,
Nuppaumukooog.
They pay not thee,
kuppaumukooog.
They pay not him,
mat uppaumouh.
They pay not us,
nuppaumukoounonog.
They pay not you,
kuppaumukoooog.
They pay not them,
mat uppaumouh.

3 *plur.*

G

Indicative

Indicative Mode.

Present tense.

1 plur.
We keep not thee,
Koowadchanunoomun.
We keep not him,
mat noowadchanóun.
We keep not you,
koowadchanunoomun.
We keep not them,
mat noowadchanounonog.

2 plur.
Ye keep not me,
Koowadchaneumwoo.
Ye keep not him,
mat koowadchanau.
Ye keep not us,
koowadchaneumun.
Ye keep not them,
mat koowadchanoog.

3 plur.
They keep not me,
Noowadchanukooog.
They keep not thee,
koowadchanukooog.
They keep not him,
mat oowadchanouh.
They keep not us,
noowadchanukoounonog.
They keep not you,
koowadchanukoooog.
They keep not them,
mat oowadchanouh.

Present tense.

1 plur.
We pay not thee,
Kuppaumunoomun.
We pay not him,
mat nuppaumoun.
We pay not you,
kuppaumunoomun.
We pay not them,
mat nuppaumounonog.

2 plur.
Ye pay not me,
Kuppaumeumwoo.
Ye pay not him,
mat kuppaumau.
Ye pay not us,
kuppaumeumun.
Ye pay not them,
mat kuppaumoog.

3 plur.
They pay not me,
Nuppaumukooog.
They pay not thee,
kuppaumukooog.
They pay not him,
mat uppaumouh.
They pay not us,
nuppaumukoounonog.
They pay not you,
kuppaumukoooog.
They pay not them,
mat uppaumouh.

Indicative Mode.

Præter tense.

1 *sing.*
{
I *did not keep thee,*
Koowadchanunoop.
I *did not keep him,*
mat noowadchanóhp.
I *did not keep you,*
koowadchanunoomwop.
I *did not keep them,*
mat noowadchanopanneg.
}

Præter tense.

1 *sing.*
{
I *did not pay thee,*
Kuppaumunoop.
I *did not pay him,*
mat nuppaumóp.
I *did not pay you,*
kuppaumunoomwop.
I *did not pay them,*
mat nuppaumopanneg.
}

2 *sing.*
{
Thou didst not keep me,
Koowadchaneup.
Thou didst not keep him,
mat koowadchanóp.
Thou didst not keep us,
koowadchaneumunonup.
Thou didst not keep them,
mat koowadchanopanneg.
}

2 *sing.*
{
Thou didst not pay me,
Kuppaumoop.
Thou didst not pay him,
mat kuppaumóp.
Thou didst not pay us,
kuppaumeumunonup.
Thou didst not pay them,
mat kuppaumopanneg.
}

3 *sing.*
{
He did not keep me,
Noowadchanukoop.
He did not keep thee,
koowadchanukoop.
He did not keep him,
mat oowadchanópoh.
He did not keep us,
noowadchanukoounonup.
He did not keep you,
koowadchanukoop.
He did not keep them,
mat oowadchanopoh.
}

3 *sing.*
{
He did not pay me,
Nuppaumukoop.
He did not pay thee,
kuppaumukoop.
He did not pay him,
mat paumópoh.
He did not pay us,
nuppaumukoounonup.
He did not pay you,
kuppaumukoop.
He did not pay them,
mat uppaumopoh.
}

Indicative

Indicative Mode.

Præter tense.

1 sing.
{
I did not keep thee,
Koowadchanunoop.
I did not keep him,
mat noowadchanóhp.
I did not keep you,
koowadchanunoomwop.
I did not keep them,
mat noowadchanopanneg.
}

2 sing.
{
Thou didst not keep me,
Koowadchaneup.
Thou didst not keep him,
mat koowadchanóp.
Thou didst not keep us,
koowadchaneumunonup.
Thou didst not keep them,
mat koowadchanopanneg.
}

3 sing.
{
He did not keep me,
Noowadchanukoop.
He did not keep thee,
koowadchanukoop.
He did not keep him,
mat oowadchanópoh.
He did not keep us,
noowadchanukoounonup.
He did not keep you,
koowadchanukooop.
He did not keep them,
mat oowadchanopoh.
}

Præter tense.

1 sing.
{
I did not pay thee,
Kuppaumunoop.
I did not pay him,
mat nuppaumóp.
I did not pay you,
kuppaumunoomwop.
I did not pay them,
mat nuppaumopanneg.
}

2 sing.
{
Thou didst not pay me,
Kuppaumoop.
Thou didst not pay him,
mat kuppaumóp.
Thou didst not pay us,
kuppaumeumunonup.
Thou didst not pay them,
mat kuppaumopanneg.
}

3 sing.
{
He did not pay me,
Nuppaumukoop.
He did not pay thee,
kuppaumukoop.
He did not pay him,
mat paumópoh.
He did not pay us,
nuppaumukoounonup.
He did not pay you,
kuppaumukooop.
He did not pay them,
mat uppaumopoh.
}

Indicative Mode.

Prater tense.   *Prater tense.*

1 plur.

We did not keep thee,
Koowadchaninoomunonup.
We did not keep him,
mat noowadchanounonup.
We did not keep you,
koowadchaninoomunonup.
We did not keep them,
mat noowadchanounonup-
(panneg.

We did not pay thee,
Kuppaumunoomunonup.
We did not pay him,
mat nuppaumóunonup.
We did not pay you,
kuppaumunoomunonup.
We did not pay them,
mat nuppaumounonuppãneg

2 plur.

Ye did not keep me,
Koowadchaneumwop.
Ye did not keep him,
mat koowadchanooop.
Ye did not keep us,
koowadchaneumunonup.
Ye did not keep them,
mat koowadchanoopanneg.

Ye did not pay me,
Kuppaumeumwop.
Ye did not pay him,
mat kuppaumooop.
Ye did not pay us,
kuppaumeumunonup.
Ye did not pay them,
mat kuppaumoopanneg.

3 plur.

They did not keep me,
Noowadchanukoopanneg.
They did not keep thee,
koowadchanukoopanneg.
They did not keep him,
mat oowadchanooopoh.
They did not keep us, (neg.
noowadchanukoounonuppan.
They did not keep you,
koowadchanukoooopanneg.
They did not keep them,
mat oowadchanooopoh.

They did not pay me,
Nuppaumukoopanneg.
They did not pay thee,
kuppaumukoopanneg.
They did not pay him,
mat uppaumooopuh.
They did not pay us,
nuppaumukoounonuppanneg
They did not pay you,
kuppaumukoóópanneg.
They did not pay them,
mat uppaumooopoh.

G 2   The

Indicative Mode.

Præter tense.

1 plur. {
We did not keep thee,
Koowadchaninoomunonup.
We did not keep him,
mat noowadchanounonup.
Wedid not keep you,
koowadchaninoomunonup.
We did not keep them,
mat noowadchanounonup-
(panneg.
}

2 plur. {
Ye did not keep me,
Koowadchaneumwop.
Ye did not keep him,
mat koowadchanooop.
Ye did not keep us,
koowadchaneumunonup.
Ye did not keep them,
mat koowadchanoopanneg.
}

3 plur. {
They did not keep me,
Noowadchanukoopanneg.
They did not keep thee,
koowadchanukoopanneg.
They did not keep him,
mat oowadchanooopoh.
They did not keep us, (neg.
noowadchanukoounonuppan-
They did not keep you,
koowadchanukoooopanneg.
They did not keep them,
mat oowadchanooopoh.
}

Præter tense.

1 plur. {
We did not pay thee,
Kuppaumunoomunonup.
We did not pay him,
mat nuppaumóunonup.
We did not pay you,
kuppaumunoomunonup.
We did not pay them,
mat nuppaumounonuppaneg.
}

2 plur. {
Ye did not pay me,
Kuppaumeumwop.
Ye did not pay him,
mat kuppaumooop.
Ye did not pay us,
kuppaumeumunonup.
Ye did not pay them,
mat kuppaumooopanneg.
}

3 plur. {
They did not pay me,
Nuppaumukoopanneg.
They did not pay thee,
kuppaumukoopanneg.
They did not pay him,
mat uppaumooopuh.
They did not pay us,
nuppaumukoounonuppanneg.
They did not pay you,
kuppaumukooóopanneg.
They did not pay them,
mat uppaumooopoh.
}

The *Suffix form Animate* Negative.

Imperative Mode.

Prefent tenfe.

1 *fing.*
{
Let me not keep thee,
Wadchanunœutti.
Let me not keep him,
wadchanoonti.
Let me not keep you,
wadchanunonkqutti.
Let me not keep them,
wadchanoonti.
}

Prefent tenfe.

1 *fing.*
{
Let me not pay thee.
Paumunutti.
Let me not pay him.
paumoonti.
Let me not pay you,
paumunœutti.
Let me not pay them,
paumoonti.
}

2 *fing.*
{
Do thou not keep me,
Wadchanohkon.
Do thou not keep him,
wadchanuhkon.
Do thou not keep us,
wadchanéittuh.
Do thou not keep them,
wadchanuhkon.
}

2 *fing.*
{
Do thou not pay me,
Paumehkon.
Do thou not pay him,
paumuhkon.
Do thou not pay us,
pauméittuh.
Do thou not pay them,
paumóhkon.
}

3 *fing.*
{
Let not him keep me,
Wadchanehkitch.
Let not him keep thee,
wadchanukœhkon.
Let not him keep him,
wadchanuhkitch.
Let not him keep us,
wadchanukœuttuh.
Let not him keep you,
wadchanukœhteók.
Let not him keep them,
wadchanuhkitch.
}

3 *fing.*
{
Let not him pay me,
Paumehkitch.
Let not him pay thee,
paumukœhkon.
Let not him pay him,
paumuhkitch.
Let not him pay us,
paumukœuttuh.
Let not him pay you,
paumukœhteók.
Let not him pay them,
paumuhkitch.
}

Imperative

The *Suffix form Animate* Negative.

Imperative Mode.

Present tense.

1 sing.
Let me not keep thee,
Wadchanunꝏutti.
Let me not keep him,
wadchanoonti.
Let me not keep you,
wadchanunonkqutti.
Let me not keep them,
wadchanoonti.

2 sing.
Do thou not keep me,
Wadchanohkon.
Do thou not keep him,
wadchanuhkon.
Do thou not keep us,
wadchanéittuh.
Do thou not keep them,
wadchanuhkon.

3 sing.
Let not him keep me,
Wadchanehkitch.
Let not him keep thee,
wadchanukꝏhkon.
Let not him keep him,
wadchanuhkitch.
Let not him keep us,
wadchanukꝏuttuh.
Let not him keep you,
wadchanukꝏhteók.
Let not him keep them,
wadchanuhkitch.

Present tense.

1 sing.
Let me not pay thee,
Paumunutti.
Let me not pay him,
paumoonti.
Let me not pay you,
paumunꝏutti.
Let me not pay them,
paumoonti.

2 sing.
Do thou not pay me,
Paumehkon.
Do thou not pay him,
paumuhkon.
Do thou not pay us,
pauméittuh.
Do thou not pay them,
paumóhkon.

3 sing.
Let not him pay me,
Paumehkitch.
Let not him pay thee,
paumukꝏhkon.
Let not him pay him,
paumuhkitch.
Let not him pay us,
paumukꝏuttuh.
Let not him pay you,
paumukꝏhteók.
Let not him pay them,
paumuhkitch.

Imperative Mode.

Prefent tenfe.

Prefent tenfe.

1 plur.

Let not us keep thee,
Wadchanunꝏuttuh.
Let not us keep him,
wadchanòontuh.
Let not us keep you,
wadchanunꝏuttuh.
Let not us keep them,
wadchanoontuh.

1 plur.

Let not us pay thee,
Paumunꝏuttuh.
Let not us pay him,
paumoontuh.
Let not us pay you,
paumunꝏuttuh.
Let not us pay them,
paumoontuh.

2 plur.

Do not ye keep me,
Wadchanehteók.
Do not ye keep him,
wadchanuhteók.
Do not ye keep us,
wadchanéinnean.
Do not ye keep them,
wadchanuhteók.

2 plur.

Do not ye pay me,
Paumehteok.
Do not ye pay him,
paumuhteok.
Do not ye pay us,
pauméinnean.
Do not ye pay them,
paumuhteok.

3 plur.

Let not them keep me,
Wadchanehettekitch.
Let not them keep thee,
wadchanukꝏhkon.
Let not them keep him,
wadchanahettekitch.
Let not them keep us,
wadchanukꝏuttuh.
Let not them keep you,
wadchanukꝏhteok.
Let not them keep them,
wadchanahettekitch.

3 plur.

Let not them pay me,
Paumehettekitch.
Let not them pay thee,
paumukꝏhkon.
Let not them pay him,
paumahettekitch.
Let not them pay us,
paumukꝏuttuh.
Let not them pay you,
paumukꝏhteok.
Let not them pay them,
paumahettekitch.

G 3

The

Imperative Mode.

Present tense.   *Present tense.*

1 *plur.* {
Let not us keep thee,
Wadchanunꝏuttuh.
Let not us keep him,
wadchanòontuh.
Let not us keep you,
wadchanunꝏuttuh.
Let not us keep them,
wadchanoontuh.
}

1 *plur.* {
Let not us pay thee,
Paumunꝏuttuh.
Let not us pay him,
paumoontuh.
Let not us pay you,
paumunꝏuttuh.
Let not us pay them,
paumoontuh.
}

2 *plur.* {
Do not ye keep me,
Wadchanehteók.
Do not ye keep him,
wadchanuhteók.
Do not ye keep us,
wadchanéinnean.
Do not ye keep them,
wadchanuhteók.
}

2 *plur.* {
Do not ye pay me,
Paumehteok.
Do not ye pay him,
paumuhteok.
Do not ye pay us,
pauméinnean.
Do not ye pay them,
paumuhteok.
}

3 *plur.* {
Let not them keep me,
Wadchanehettekitch.
Let not them keep thee,
wadchanukꝏhkon.
Let not them keep him,
wadchanahettekitch.
Let not them keep us,
wadchanukꝏuttuh.
Let not them keep you,
wadchanukꝏhteok.
Let not them keep them,
wadchanahettekitch.
}

3 *plur.* {
Let not them pay me,
Paumehettekitch.
Let not them pay thee,
paumukꝏhkon.
Let not them pay him,
paumahettekitch.
Let not them pay us,
paumukꝏuttuh.
Let not them pay you,
paumukꝏhteok.
Let not them pay them,
paumahettekitch.
}

The *Suffix form Animate* Negative.

Optative Mode.

Present tense.	*Present tense.*

1 sing.

I wish I keep not thee,
Koowaadchanunꝏoun-toh.
I wish I keep not him,
noowaadchanoun-toh.
I wish I keep not you,
koowaadchanunꝏouneau-toh.
I wish I keep not them,
noowaadchanouneau-toh.

1 sing.

I wish I do not pay thee,
Kuppapaumunꝏoun-toh.
I wish I do not pay him,
nuppapaumoon-toh.
I wish I do not pay you,
kuppapaumunꝏouneau-toh.
I wish I do not pay them,
nuppapaumouneau-toh.

2 sing.

I wish thou do not keep me,
Koowaadchanein-toh.
I wish thou do not keep him,
koowaadchanoon-toh.
I wish thou do not keep us,
koowaadchanein-toh.
I wish thou do not keep them,
koowaadchanouneau-toh.

2 sing.

I wish thou do not pay me,
Kuppapauméin-toh.
I wish thou do not pay him,
kuppapaumoon-toh.
I wish thou do not pay us,
kuppapauméinan-toh.
I wish thou no not pay them,
kuppapaumouneau-toh.

3 sing.

I wish he do not keep me,
Noowaadchanukꝏoun-toh.
I wish he do not keep thee,
koowaadchanukꝏoun-toh.
I wish he do not keep him,
ꝏwaadchanoon-toh.
I wish he do not keep us,
noowaadchanukꝏunan-toh.
I wish he do not keep you,
koowaadchanukꝏouneau-toh,
I wish he do not keep them,
ꝏwaadchanoon-toh.

3 sing.

I wish he do not pay me,
Nuppapaumukꝏoun-toh.
I wish he do not pay thee,
kuppapaumukꝏoun-toh.
I wish he do not pay him
uppapaumoun-toh.
I wish he do not pay us,
nuppapaumukꝏunan-toh.
I wish he do not pay you,
kuppapaumukꝏouneau-toh.
I wish he do not pay them,
uppapaumouneau-toh.

Optative

The *Suffix form Animate* Negative.

Optative Mode.

Present tense.

I sing. {
I wish I keep not thee,
Kœwaadchanunœun-toh.
I wish I keep not him,
nœwaadchanoun-toh.
I wish I keep not you,
kœwaadchanunœuneau-toh.
I wish I keep not them,
nœwaadchanouneau-toh.
}

2 sing. {
I wish thou do not keep me,
Kœwaadchanein-toh.
I wish thou do not keep him,
kœwaadchanoon-toh.
I wish thou do not keep us,
kœwaadchanein-toh.
I wish thou do not keep them,
kœwaadchanouneau-toh.
}

3 sing. {
I wish he do not keep me,
Nœwaadchanukœun-toh.
I wish he do not keep thee,
kœwaadchanukœun-toh.
I wish he do not keep him,
œwaadchanoon-toh.
I wish he do not keep us,
nœwaadchanukœunan-toh.
I wish he do not keep you,
kœwaadchanukœuneau-toh.
I wish he do not keep them,
œwaadchanoon-toh.
}

Present tense.

I sing. {
I wish I pay not thee,
Kuppapaumunœun-toh.
I wish I pay not him,
nuppapaumoon-toh.
I wish I pay not you,
kuppapaumunœuneau-toh.
I wish I pay not them,
nuppapaumouneau-toh.
}

2 sing. {
I wish thou do not pay me,
Kuppapauméin-toh.
I wish thou do not pay him,
kuppapaumoon-toh.
I wish thou do not pay us,
kuppapauméinan-toh.
I wish thou do not pay them,
kuppapaumouneau-toh.
}

3 sing. {
I wish he do not pay me,
Nuppapaumukœun-toh.
I wish he do not pay thee,
kuppapaumukœun-toh.
I wish he do not pay him,
uppapaumoun-toh.
I wish he do not pay us,
nuppapaumukœunan-toh.
I wish he do not pay you,
kuppapaumukœuneau-toh.
I wish he do not pay them,
uppapaumouneau-toh.
}

Optative Mode.

I wish we do not keep thee,
Koowaadchananoounan-toh.
I wish we do not keep him,
noowaadchanounan-toh.
I wish we do not keep you,
koowaadchanounan-toh.
I wish we do not keep them,
noowaadchanounan--toh.

1 *plur.*

I wish ye do not keep me,
Koowaadchaneinneau-toh.
I wish ye do not keep him,
koowaadchanouneau-toh.
I wish ye do not keep us,
koowaadchanéinnean-toh.
I wish ye do not keep them,
koowaadchanouneau-toh.

2 *plur.*

I wish they do not keep me,
Noowaadchanukoouneau-toh.
I wish they do not keep thee,
koowaadchanukoouneau-toh.
I wish they do not keep him,
oowaadchanouneau-toh.
I wish they do not keep us,
noowaadchanukoounan-toh.
I wish they do not keep you,
koowaadchanukoouneau-toh.
I wish they do not keep them,
oowaadchanouneau-toh.

3 *plur.*

I wish we do not pay thee,
Kuppapaumunoooon-toh.
I wish we do not pay him,
nuppapaumoon-toh.
I wish we do not pay you,
kuppapaumunoounan-toh.
I wish we do not pay them,
nuppapaumounan-toh.

1 *plur.*

I wish ye do not pay me,
Kuppapauméineau-toh.
I wish ye do not pay him,
kuppapaumooneau-toh.
I wish ye do not pay us,
kuppapauméinan-toh.
I wish ye do not pay them,
kuppapaumooneau-toh.

2 *plur.*

I wish they do not pay me,
Nuppapaumukoouneau-toh.
I wish they do not pay thee,
kuppapaumukoouneau-toh.
I wish they do not pay him,
uppapaumouneau-toh.
I wish they do not pay us,
nuppapaumukoounan-toh.
I wish they do not pay you,
kuppapaumukoouneau--toh.
I wish they do not pay them,
uppapaumouneau-toh.

3 *plur.*

Optative Mode.

Present tense.

1 plur. {
I wish we do not keep thee,
Koowaadchananoounan-toh.
I wish we do not keep him,
noowaadchanounan-toh.
I wish we do not keep you,
koowaadchanounan-toh.
I wish we do not keep them,
noowaadchanounan-toh.
}

2 plur. {
I wish ye do not keep me,
Koowaadchaneinneau-toh.
I wish ye do not keep him,
koowaadchanouneau-toh.
I wish ye do not keep us,
koowaadchanéinnean-toh.
I wish ye do not keep them,
koowaadchanouneau-toh.
}

3 plur. {
I wish they do not keep me,
Noowaadchanukoouneau-toh.
I wish they do not keep thee,
koowaadchanukoouneau-toh.
I wish they do not keep him,
oowaadchanouneau-toh.
I wish they do not keep us,
noowaadchanukoounan-toh.
I wish they do not keep you,
koowaadchanukoouneau-toh.
I wish they do not keep them,
oowaadchanouneau-toh.
}

Present tense.

1 plur. {
I wish we do not pay thee,
Kuppapaumunoooon-toh.
I wish we do not pay him,
nuppapaumoon-toh.
I wish we do not pay you,
kuppapaumunoounan-toh.
I wish we do not pay them,
nuppapaumounan-toh.
}

2 plur. {
I wish ye do not pay me,
Kuppapauméineau-toh.
I wish ye do not pay him,
kuppapaumooneau-toh.
I wish ye do not pay us,
kuppapauméinan-toh.
I wish ye do not pay them,
kuppapaumooneau-toh.
}

3 plur. {
I wish they do not pay me,
Nuppapaumukoouneau-toh.
I wish they do not pay thee,
kuppapaumukoouneau-toh.
I wish they do not pay him,
uppapaumouneau-toh.
I wish they do not pay us,
nuppapaumukoounan-toh.
I wish they do not pay you,
kuppapaumukoouneau-toh.
I wish they do not pay them,
uppapaumouneau-toh.
}

Optative Mode.

Prater tenſe.   *Prater tenſe.*

1 ſing.

I wiſh I did not keep thee,
Koowaadchanunœunaz-toh.
I wiſh I did not keep him,
noowaadchanòunaz-toh.
I Wiſh I did not keep you,
koowaadchanunounaouz-toh
I Wiſh I did not keep them,
noowaadchanòunaouz-toh.

1 ſing.

I wiſh I did not pay thee,
Kuppapaumunœunaz-toh.
I Wiſh I did not pay him,
nuppapaumounaz-toh.
I wiſh I did not pay you,
kuppapaumunœunaouz-toh.
I wiſh I did not pay them,
nuppapaumounaouz-toh.

2 ſing.

I wiſh thou didſt not keep me,
Koowaadchanéinaz-toh.
I wiſh thou didſt not keep him,
koowaadchanóunaz-toh.
I wiſh thou didſt not keep us,
koowaadchaneinanonaz-toh.
I wiſh thou didſt not keep them,
koowaadchanounnaouz-toh.

2 ſing.

I wiſh thou didſt not pay me,
Kuppapauméinaz-toh.
I wiſh thou didſt not pay him,
kuppapaumounaz-toh.
I wiſh thou didſt not pay us,
kuppapauméinanonuz-toh.
I Wiſh thou didſt not pay them,
kuppapaumounaouz-toh.

3 ſing.

I wiſh he did not keep me,
Noowaadchanukœunuz-toh.
I wiſh he did not keep thee,
koowaadchanukœunaz-toh.
I wiſh he did not keep him,
oowaadchanounaz-toh.
I wiſh he did not keep us, (toh
noowaadchanukœunanonuz-
I wiſh he did not keep you,
koowaadchanykœaunouz-toh
I wiſh he did not keep them,
oowaadchanòunaouz--toh.

3 ſing.

I Wiſh he did not pay me,
Nuppapaumukœunaz--toh.
I wiſh he did not pay thee,
kuppapaumukœunaz-toh.
I wiſh he did not pay him,
uppapaumóunaz-toh.
I wiſh he did not pay us,
nuppapaumukœouanonuz-toh.
I wiſh he did not pay you,
kuppapaumukœunaouz-toh.
I Wiſh he did not pay them,
uppapaumounaz-toh.

Optative Mode.

Præter tense.

1 *sing.*
{
I wish I did not keep thee,
Koowaadchanunoounaz-toh.
I wish I did not keep him,
noowaadchanòunaz-toh.
I wish I did not keep you,
koowaadchanunounaouz-toh.
I wish I did not keep them,
noowaadchanòunaouz-toh.
}

Præter tense.

1 *sing.*
{
I wish I did not pay thee,
Kuppapaumunoounaz-toh.
I wish I did not pay him,
nuppapaumounaz-toh.
I wish I did not pay you,
kuppapaumunoounaouz-toh.
I wish I did not pay them,
nuppapaumounaouz-toh.
}

2 *sing.*
{
I wish thou didst not keep me,
Koowaadchanéinaz-toh.
I wish thou didst not keep him,
koowaadchanóunaz-toh.
I wish thou didst not keep us,
koowaadchaneinanonaz-toh.
I wish thou didst not keep them,
koowaadchanounnaouz-toh.
}

2 *sing.*
{
I wish thou didst not pay me,
Kuppapauméinaz-toh.
I wish thou didst not pay him,
kuppapaumounaz-toh.
I wish thou didst not pay us,
kuppapauméinanonuz-toh.
I wish thou didst not pay them,
kuppapaumounaouz-toh.
}

3 *sing.*
{
I wish he did not keep me,
Noowaadchanukoounaz-toh.
I wish he did not keep thee,
koowaadchanukoounaz-toh.
I wish he did not keep him,
oowaadchanounaz-toh.
I wish he did not keep us,
noowaadchanukoounanonuz-toh.
I wish he did not keep you,
koowaadchanukooaunaz-toh.
I wish he did not keep them,
oowaadchanòunaouz-toh.
}

3 *sing.*
{
I wish he did not pay me,
Nuppapaumukoounaz-toh.
I wish he did not pay thee,
kuppapaumukoounaz-toh.
I wish he did not pay him,
uppapaumóunaz-toh.
I wish he did not pay us,
nuppapaumukoounanonuz-toh.
I wish he did not pay you,
kuppapaumukoounaouz-toh.
I wish he did not pay them,
uppapaumounaz-toh.
}

Optative Mode.

Præter tenſe.

1 plur.
{
I wiſh we did not keep thee,
koowaadchanunooúnanonuz-toh
I wiſh we did not keep him,
noowaadchanoúnanonuz-toh.
I wiſh we did not keep you,
koowaadchanooúnaouz-toh
I wiſh we did not keep them,
noowaadchanooúnaouz-toh.
}

plur.
{
I wiſh ye did not keep me,
Koowaadchanéinaouz-toh.
I wiſh ye did not keep him,
koowaadchanounaouz-toh.
I wiſh ye did not keep us,
koowaadchanéinanonaz-toh.
I wiſh ye did not keep them,
koowaadchanounnaouz-toh.
}

3 plur.
{
I wiſh they did not keep me,
Noowaadchanukooúnaz-toh.
I wiſh they did not keep thee,
koowaadchanukooúnaz-toh.
I wiſh they did not keep him,
oowaadchanoúnaoaz-toh.
I wiſh they did not keep us,
noowaadchanukooúnanonaz-toh
I wiſh they did not keep you,
koowaadchanukooúnaouz-toh.
I wiſh they did not keep them,
oowaadchanoúnaoaz-toh.
}

Præter tenſe.

1 plur.
{
I wiſh we did not pay thee,
kuppapaumunooúanonuz-toh
I wiſh we did not pay him,
nuppapaumounanonuz-toh.
I wiſh we did not pay you,
kuppapaumunooúnaoaz-toh.
I wiſh we did not pay them,
nuppapaumounaoaz-toh.
}

2 plur.
{
I wiſh ye did not pay me,
Kuppapauméinaoaz-toh.
I wiſh ye did not pay him,
kuppapaumoonaoaz-toh.
I wiſh ye did not pay us,
kuppapauméinnanonaz-toh.
I wiſh ye did not pay them,
kuppapaumoonaoaz-toh.
}

3 plur.
{
I wiſh they did not pay me,
Nuppapaumukooúnaooz-toh.
I wiſh they did not pay thee,
kuppapaumukooúnaooz-toh.
I wiſh they did not pay him,
uppapaumoonaz-toh.
I wiſh they did not pay us,
nuppapaumukooúanonaz-toh.
I wiſh they did not pay you,
kuppapaumukooúnaoaz-toh.
I wiſh they did not pay them,
uppapaumounaoaz-toh.
}

H   The

Optative Mode.

Præter tense.

1 plur.
I wish we did not keep thee,
koowaadchanunœunanonuz-toh.
I wish we did not keep him,
noowaadchanounanonuz-toh.
I wish we did not keep you,
koowaadchanœunaouz-toh.
I wish we did not keep them,
noowaadchanœunaouz-toh.

2 plur.
I wish ye did not keep me,
Koowaadchanéinaouz-toh.
I wish ye did not keep him,
koowaadchanounaouz-toh.
I wish ye did not keep us,
koowaadchanéinanonaz-toh.
I wish ye did not keep them,
koowaadchanounnaonuz-toh.

3 plur.
I wish they did not keep me,
Noowaadchanukœunaz-toh.
I wish they did not keep thee,
koowaadchanukœunaz-toh.
I wish they did not keep him,
œwaadchanounaoaz-toh.
I wish they did not keep us,
noowaadchanukœunanonaz-toh.
I wish they did not keep you,
koowaadchanukœunaouz-toh.
I wish they did not keep them,
œwaadchanounaoaz-toh.

Præter tense.

1 plur.
I wish we did not pay thee,
kuppapaumunœuanonuz-toh.
I wish we did not pay him,
nuppapaumounanonuz-toh.
I wish we did not pay you,
kuppapaumunœunaoaz-toh.
I wish we did not pay them,
nuppapaumounaoaz-toh.

2 plur.
I wish ye did not pay me,
Kuppapauméinaoaz-toh.
I wish ye did not pay him,
kuppapaumoonaoaz-toh.
I wish ye did not pay us,
kuppapauméinnanonaz-toh.
I wish ye did not pay them,
kuppapaumoonaoaz-toh.

3 plur.
I wish they did not pay me,
Nuppapaumukœunaooz-toh.
I wish they did not pay thee,
kuppapaumukœunaooz-toh.
I wish they did not pay him,
uppapaumoonaz-toh.
I wish they did not pay us,
nuppapaumukœuanonaz-toh.
I wish they did not pay you,
kuppapaumukœunaoaz-toh.
I wish they did not pay them,
uppapaumounaoaz-toh.

The *Suffix form Animate* Negative.

Suppositive Mode.

Present tense.   *Present tense.*

1 *sing.* {
 If I keep not thee,
Wadchanuncoon.
 If I keep not him,
wadchanoog.
 If I keep not you,
wadchanuncoog.
 If I keep not them,
wadchanoog.
}

1 *sing.* {
 If I pay not thee,
Paumuncoon.
 If I pay not him,
paumoog.
 If I pay not you,
paumuncoog.
 If I pay not them
paumoog.
}

2 *sing.* {
 If thou keep not me,
Wadchaneean.
 If thou keep not him,
wadchanoadt.
 If thou keep not us,
wadchaneeog.
 If I keep not them,
wadchanoadt.
}

2 *sing.* {
 If thou pay not me,
Paumeean.
 If I pay not him,
paumoadt.
 If thou pay not us,
paumeeog.
 If thou pay not them,
paumoadt.
}

3 *sing.* {
 If he keep not me,
Wadchaneegk.
 If he keep not thee,
wadchanukcoan.
 If he keep not him,
wadchanunk.
 If he keep not us,
wadchanukcoog.
 If he keep not you,
wadchanukcoóg.
 If he keep not them,
wadchanunk.
}

3 *sing.* {
 If he pay not me,
Paumeegk.
 If he pay not thee,
paumukcoan.
 If he pay not him,
paumunk.
 If he pay not us,
paumukcoog.
 If he pay not you,
paumukcoog.
 If he pay not them,
paumunk.
}

Suppositive

The *Suffix form Animate* Negative.

Suppositive Mode.

Present tense.   *Present tense.*

1 sing.
{
If I *keep* not thee,
Wadchanunꝏon.
If I *keep* not him,
wadchanoog.
If I *keep* not you,
wadchanunꝏog.
If I *keep* not them,
wadchanoog.
}

1 sing.
{
If I pay not thee,
Paumunꝏon.
If I pay not him,
paumoog.
If I pay not you,
paumunꝏog.
If I pay not them,
paumoog.
}

2 sing.
{
If thou *keep* not me,
Wadchaneean.
If thou *keep* not him,
wadchanoadt.
If thou *keep* not us,
wadchaneeog.
If thou *keep* not them,
wadchanoadt.
}

2 sing.
{
If thou pay not me,
Paumeean.
If thou pay not him,
paumoadt.
If thou pay not us,
paumeeog.
If thou pay not them,
paumoadt.
}

3 sing.
{
If he *keep* not me,
Wadchaneegk.
If he *keep* not thee,
wadchanukꝏan.
If he *keep* not him,
wadchanunk.
If he *keep* not us,
wadchanukꝏog.
If he *keep* not you,
wadchanukꝏóg.
If he *keep* not them,
wadchanunk.
}

3 sing.
{
If he pay not me,
Paumeegk.
If he pay not thee,
paumukꝏan.
If he pay not him,
paumunk.
If he pay not us,
paumukꝏog.
If he pay not you,
paumukꝏog.
If he pay not them,
paumunk.
}

Suppofitive Mode.

Prefent tenfe.

1 plur.
{
If we keep not thee,
Wadchanunꝏog.
If we keep not him,
wadchanoogkut.
If we keep not you,
wadchanunꝏog.
If we keep not them,
wadchanoogkut.
}

2 plur.
{
If ye keep not me,
Wadchaneeóg.
If ye keep not him,
wadchanoóg.
If ye keep not us,
wadchaneeog.
If ye keep not them,
wadchanoóg.
}

3 plur.
{
If they keep not me,
Wadchanehetteg.
If they keep not thee,
wadchanukꝏan.
If they keep not him,
wadchanahetteg.
If they keep not us,
wadchanukꝏog.
If they keep not you,
wadchanukꝏóg.
If they keep not them,
wadchanahetteg.
}

Prefent tenfe.

1 plur.
{
If we pay not thee,
Paumunꝏog.
If we pay not him,
paumoogkut.
If we pay not you,
paumunꝏóg.
If we pay not them,
paumoogkut.
}

2 plur.
{
If ye pay not me,
Paumeeóg.
If ye pay not him,
paumôóg.
If ye pay not us,
paumeeòg.
If ye pay not them,
paumôóg.
}

3 plur.
{
If they pay not me,
Paumehetteg.
If they pay not thee,
paumukꝏan.
If they pay not him,
paumahetteg.
If they pay not us,
paumukꝏog.
If they pay not you,
paumukꝏog.
If they pay not them,
paumahetteg.
}

Suppofitive

Suppositive Mode.

Present tense.   *Present tense.*

1 plur.
- If we keep not thee, Wadchanunꝏog.
- If we keep not him, wadchanoogkut.
- If we keep not you, wadchanunꝏog.
- If we keep not them, wadchanoogkut.

1 plur.
- If we pay not thee, Paumunꝏog.
- If we pay not him, paumoogkut.
- If we pay not you, paumunꝏóg.
- If we pay not them, paumoogkut.

2 plur.
- If ye keep not me, Wadchaneeóg.
- If ye keep not him, wadchanoóg.
- If ye keep not us, wadchaneeog.
- If ye keep not them, wadchanoóg.

2 plur.
- If ye pay not me, Paumeeòg.
- If ye pay not him, paumôòg.
- If ye pay not us, paumeeòg.
- If ye pay not them, paumôòg.

3 plur.
- If they keep not me, Wadchanehetteg.
- If they keep not thee, wadchanukꝏan.
- If they keep not him, wadchanahetteg.
- If they keep not us, wadchanukꝏog.
- If they keep not you, wadchanukꝏóg.
- If they keep not them, wadchanahetteg.

3 plur.
- If they pay not me, Paumehetteg.
- If they pay not thee, paumukꝏan.
- If they pay not him, paumahetteg.
- If they pay not us, paumukꝏog.
- If they pay not you, paumukꝏog.
- If they pay not them, paumahetteg.

Suppofitive Mode.

Prater tenfe.

1 sing.
{ If I did not keep thee,
Wadchanunꝏos.
If I did not keep him,
wadchanoogkus.
If I did not keep you,
wadchanunꝏógkus.
If I did not keep them,
wadchanoogkus.

2 sing.
{ If thou didſt not keep me,
Wadchaneeas.
If thou didſt not keep him,
wadchanoas.
If thou didſt not keep us,
wadchaneeogkus.
If thou didſt not keep them,
wadchanoògkus.

3 sing.
{ If he did not keep me,
Wadchàneekus.
If he did not keep thee,
wadchanukꝏas.
If he did not keep him,
wadchanunkus.
If he did not keep us,
wadchanukꝏꝏogkus.
If he did not keep you,
wadchanukogkus.
If he did not keep them,
wadchanunkus.

Prater tenfe.

1 sing.
{ If I did not pay thee,
Paumunꝏos.
If I did not pay him,
paumoogkus.
If I did not pay you,
paumunꝏógkus.
If I did not pay them,
paumoogkus.

2 sing.
{ If thou didſt not pay me,
Paumeeas.
If thou didſt not pay him,
paumoas.
If thou didſt not pay us,
paumeeogkus.
If thou didſt not pay them,
paumoógkus.

3 sing.
{ If he did not pay me,
Paumeekus.
If he did not pay thee,
paumukꝏas.
If he did not pay him,
paumunkus.
If he did not pay us,
paumukꝏogkus.
If he did not pay you,
paumukꝏógkus.
If he did not pay them,
paumunkus.

Suppofitive

Suppositive Mode.

Præter tense.

1 sing.

If I did not keep thee,
Wadchanunꝏos.
If I did not keep him,
wadchanoogkus.
If I did not keep you,
wadchanunꝏógkus.
If I did not keep them,
wadchanoogkus.

2 sing.

If thou didst not keep me,
Wadchaneeas.
If thou didst not keep him,
wadchanoas.
If thou didst not keep us,
wadchaneeogkus.
If thou didst not keep them,
wadchanoògkus.

3 sing.

If he did not keep me,
Wadchàneekus.
If he did not keep thee,
wadchanukꝏas.
If he did not keep him,
wadchanunkus.
If he did not keep us,
wadchanukꝏꝏogkus.
If he did not keep you,
wadchanukogkus.
If he did not keep them,
wadchanunkus.

Præter tense.

1 sing.

If I did not pay thee,
Paumunꝏos.
If I did not pay him,
paumoogkus.
If I did not pay you,
paumunꝏógkus.
If I did not pay them,
paumoogkus.

2 sing.

If thou didst not pay me,
Paumeeas.
If thou didst not pay him,
paumoas.
If thou didst not pay us,
paumeeogkus.
If thou didst not pay them,
paumoógkus.

3 sing.

If he did not pay me,
Paumeekus.
If he did not pay thee,
paumukꝏas.
If he did not pay him,
paumunkus.
If he did not pay us,
paumukꝏogkus.
If he did not pay you,
paumukꝏógkus.
If he did not pay them,
paumunkus.

Suppofitive Mode.

Præter tenfe.   *Præter tenfe.*

1 plur.

If *we did not keep thee,*
Wadchanunꝏogkus.
    If *we did not keep him,*
wadchanoogkutus.
    If *we did not keep you,*
wadchanunꝏógkus.
    If *we did not keep them,*
wadchanoogkutus.

1 plur.

If *we did not pay thee,*
Paumunꝏogkus.
    If *we did not pay him,*
paumoogkutus.
    If *we did not pay you,*
paumunꝏógkus.
    If *we did not pay them,*
paumoogkutus.

2 plur.

If *ye did not keep me,*
Wadchaneeógkus.
    If *ye did not keep him,*
wadchanoógkus.
    If *ye did not keep us,*
wadchaneeogkus.
    If *ye did not keep them,*
wadchanoógkus.

2 plur.

If *ye did not pay me,*
Paumeeógkus.
    If *ye did not pay him,*
paumoógkus.
    If *ye did not pay us,*
paumeeogkus.
    If *ye did not pay them,*
paumoógkus.

3 plur.

If *they did not keep me,*
Wadchanehettegkis.
    If *they did not keep thee,*
wadchanukꝏas.
    If *they did not keep him,*
wadchanunkus.
    If *they did not keep us,*
wadchanukꝏogkus.
    If *they did not keep you,*
wadchanukꝏógkus.
    If *they did not keep them,*
wadchanahettegkis.

3 plur.

If *they did not pay me,*
Paumehettegkis.
    If *they did not pay thee,*
paumukꝏas.
    If *they did not pay him,*
paumunkus.
    If *they did not pay us,*
paumukꝏogkus.
    If *they did not pay you,*
paumukꝏógkus.
    If *they did not pay them,*
paumahettegkis.

H 3   The

Suppositive Mode.

Præter tense.   *Præter tense.*

1 *plur.* {

If we did not keep thee,
Wadchanunꝏogkus.
If we did not keep him,
waadchanoogkutus.
If we did not keep you,
wadchanunꝏógkus.
If we did not keep them,
wadchanoogkutus.

1 *plur.* {

If we did not pay thee,
Paumunꝏogkus.
If we did not pay him,
paumoogkutus.
If we did not pay you,
paumunꝏògkus.
If we did not pay them,
paumoogkutus.

2 *plur.* {

If ye did not keep me,
Wadchaneeógkus.
If ye did not keep him,
wadchanoógkus.
If ye did not keep us,
wadchaneeogkus.
If ye did not keep them,
wadchanoógkus.

2 *plur.* {

If ye did not pay me,
Paumeeógkus.
If ye did not pay him,
paumoógkus.
If ye did not pay us,
paumeeogkus.
If ye did not pay them,
paumoógkus.

3 *plur.* {

If they did not keep me,
Wadchanehettegkis.
If they did not keep thee,
wadchanukꝏas.
If they did not keep him,
wadchanunkus.
If they did not keep us,
wadchanukꝏogkus.
If they did not keep you,
wadchanukꝏógkus.
If they did not keep them,
wadchanahettegkis.

3 *plur.* {

If they did not pay me,
Paumehettegkis.
If they did not pay thee,
paumukꝏas.
If they did not pay him,
paumunkus.
If they did not pay us,
paumukꝏogkus.
If they did not pay you,
paumukꝏògkus.
If they did not pay them,
paumahettegkis.

The Indefinite Mode.

Prefent tenfe.   *Prefent tenfe.*

Not to keep,   *Not to pay,*
Wadchanounat   Paummuôunat.

The *third Perfon* of the *Suffix form Animate Negative* is found expreffible in this *Mode Indefinite* :   As

3 fing.

Not to keep me,
Noowadchanukoounat.
Not to keep thee,
koowadchanukoounat.
Not to keep him,
oowadchanounat.
Not to keep us,
noowadchanukoounnanonut.
Not to keep you,
koowadchanukoounnaout.
Not to keep them,
oowadchanounat.

3 fing.

Not to pay me,
Nuppaumunkoounat.
Not to pay thee,
kuppaumukoounat.
Not to pay him,
uppaumounat.
Not to pay us,
nuppaumukoounnanonut.
Not to pay you,
kuppaumukoounnaout.
Not to pay them,
uppaumounnaout.

So much for the Suffix form Animate Negative.

The Indefinite Mode.

Present tense.	*Present tense.*
Not to keep,	*Not to pay,*
Wadchanounat.	Paummuôunat.

The *third Person* of the *Suffix form Animate Negative* is found expressible in this *Mode Indefinite* : As

3 *sing.*
{
> *Not to keep me,*
> Nœowadchanukœounat.
> *Not to keep thee,*
> kœowadchanukœounat.
> *Not to keep him,*
> œowadchanounat.
> *Not to keep us,*
> nœowadchanukœounnanonut.
> *Not to keep you,*
> kœowadchanukœounnaout.
> *Not to keep them,*
> œowadchanounat.

3 *sing.*
{
> *Not to pay me,*
> Nuppaumunkœounat.
> *Not to pay thee,*
> kuppaumukœounat.
> *Not to pay him,*
> uppaumounat.
> *Not to pay us,*
> nuppaumukœounnanonut.
> *Not to pay you,*
> kuppaumukœounnaout.
> *Not to pay them,*
> uppaumounnaout.

So much for the Suffix form Animate Negative.

The *Suffix form Animate Caufative* is not univerfally applicable to this *Verb*; neither have I yet fully beat it out: onely in fome chief wayes of the ufe of it in Speech I fhall here fet down, leaving the reft for afterwards, if God will, and that I live to adde unto this beginning.

Affirmative.	*Negative.*
1 { *I caufe thee to keep me,* koowadchanumwahefh nuhhog *I caufe thee to keep him,* koowadchanumwahunun. *I caufe thee to keep them,* koowadchanumwahunununk.	1 { *I caufe thee not to keep me,* koowadchanûwahûooh nuhhog *I caufe thee not to keep him,* koowadchanumwahunooun. *I caufe thee not to keep them,* koowadchanumwahunoounũk
2 { *Thou makeft me keep him,* Koowadchanumwahen. *Thou makeft me keep them,* koowadchanumwáheneunk.	2 { *Thou makeft me not keep him,* Koowadchanumwahéin. *Thou makeft me not keep them,* koowadchanumwaheinunk.
3 { *He maketh me keep-him,* Noowadchanûmwahikqunuh. *He maketh me keep them,* nah noowadchanûwahikquuh	3 { *He maketh me not keep him,* noowadchanumwahikoounuh *He maketh me not keep them,* Ibid.

Imperative Mode.

{ *Make me keep him,* Wadchanumwaheh n noh. *Make me keep them,* Nah wadchanumwaheh.	{ *Make me not keep him,* Wadchanumwahehkon. *Make me not keep them,* Ibid.

Suppofitive Mode.

{ *If thou make me keep him,* Wadchanumwahean yeuoh.	{ *If thou make me not keep him,* Wadchanumwaheean.

I was

59 *The* Indian *Grammar begun.*

The *Suffix form Animate Causative* is not universally applicable to this *Verb*; neither have I yet fully beat it out : onely in some chief wayes of the use of it in Speech I shall here set down, leaving the rest for afterwards, if God will, and that I live to adde unto this beginning.

	Affirmative.	*Negative.*

1 {
I cause thee to keep me,
koowadchanumwahesh nuhhog.
I cause thee to keep him,
koowadchanumwahunun.
I cause thee to keep them,
koowadchanumwahunununk.

1 {
I cause thee not to keep me,
koowadchanúwahúoh nuhhog
I cause thee not to keep him,
koowadchanumwahunooun.
I cause thee not to keep them,
koowadchanumwahunooounúk

2 {
Thou makest me keep him,
Koowadchanumwahen.
Thou makest me keep them,
koowadchanumwáheneunk.

2 {
Thou makest me not keep him,
Koowadchanumwahéin.
Thou makest me not keep them,
koowadchanumwaheinunk.

3 {
He maketh me keep him,
Noowadchanumwahikqunuh.
He maketh me keep them,
nah noowadchanúwahikquuh

3 {
He maketh me not keep him,
noowadchanumwahikoounuh.
He maketh me not keep them,
Ibid.

Imperative Mode.

{
Make me keep him,
Wadchanumwaheh n noh.
Make me keep them,
Nah wadchanumwaheh.

{
Make me not keep him,
Wadchanumwahehkon.
Make me not keep them,
Ibid.

Suppositive Mode.

{
If thou make me keep him,
Wadchanumwahean yeuoh.

{
If thou make me not keep him,
Wadchanumwaheean.

I *Was purposed to put in no more* Paradigms *of* Verbs; *but considering that all Languages (so farre as I know) and this also, do often make use of the Verb* Substantive Passive, *and in the reason of Speech it is of frequent use: Considering also that it doth differ in its formation from other Verbs, and that Verbals are often derived out of this form, as* Wadchanittuonk, *Salvation*, &c. &c. *I have therefore here put down an Example thereof.*

The Verb Substantive Passive.

Nꝏwadchanit,   *I am kept.*

Indicative Mode.

Present tense.

sing.
{
I am kept,
Nꝏwadchanit.
Thou art kept,
kꝏwadchanit.
He is kept,
wadchanau.

Present tense.

plur.
{
We are kept,
Nꝏwadchanitteamun.
Ye are kept,
kꝏwadchanitteamwꝏ·
They are kept,
wadchanoog.

Præter tense.

sing.
{
I was kept,
Nꝏwadchanitteap.
Thou wast kept,
kꝏwadchanitteap.
He was kept,
wadchanop.

Præter tense.

plur.
{
We were kept,
Nꝏwadchanitteamunónup.
Ye were kept,
kꝏwadchanitteamwóp.
They were kept,
wadchanopanneg.

Imperative

I *Was purposed to put in no more* Paradigms *of Verbs ; but considering that all Languages (so farre as I know) and this also, do often make use of the Verb* Substantive Passive, *and in the reason of Speech it is of frequent use : Considering also that it doth differ in its formation from other Verbs, and that Verbals are often derived out of this form, as* Wadchanittuonk, Salvation, &c. &c. *I have therefore here put down an Example thereof.*

The Verb Substantive Passive.

Nꝏwadchanit,   *I am kept.*

Indicative Mode.

Present tense.   *Present tense.*

sing.
{
I am kept,
Nꝏwadchanit.
Thou art kept,
kꝏwadchanit.
He is kept,
wadchanau.

plur.
{
We are kept,
Nꝏwadchanitteamun
Ye are kept,
kꝏwadchanitteamwꝏ.
They are kept,
wadchanoog.

Præter tense.   *Præter tense.*

sing.
{
I was kept,
Nꝏwadchanitteap.
Thou wast kept,
kꝏwadchanitteap.
He was kept,
wadchanop

plur.
{
We were kept,
Nꝏwadchanitteamunónup.
Ye were kept,
kꝏwadchanitteamwóp.
They were kept,
wadchanopanneg.

Imperative Mode.

sing.
{
Let me be kept,
Wadchanitteadti.
Be thou kept,
wadchanitteaſh.
Let him be kept,
wadchanaj.
}

plur.
{
Let us be kept,
Wadchanitteatuh.
Be ye kept,
wadchanitteak.
Let them be kept,
wadchanaj.
}

Optative Mode.

Preſent tenſe.

sing.
{
I wiſh I be kept,
Nꝏwaadchanittean-toh.
I wiſh thou be kept,
kꝏwaadchanittean-toh.
I wiſh he be kept,
waadchanon-toh.
}

Preſent tenſe.

plur.
{
I wiſh we be kept,
Nꝏwaadchanitteanan-toh.
I wiſh ye be kept,
kꝏwaadchanitteaneau-toh.
I wiſh they be kept,
waadchanoneau-toh.
}

Præter tenſe.

sing.
{
I wiſh I was kept,
Nꝏwaadchanitteanaz-toh.
I wiſh thou waſt kept,
kꝏwaadchanitteanaz-toh.
I wiſh he was kept,
waadchanònaz-toh,
}

Præter tenſe.

plur.
{
I wiſh we were kept, (toh.
Nꝏwaadchanitteananȯnuz-
I wiſh ye were kept,
kꝏwaadchanitteanaouz-toh.
I wiſh they were kept,
waadchanonaouz-toh.
}

I Suppoſitive

Imperative Mode.

sing. {
Let me be kept,
Wadchanitteadti.
Be thou kept,
wadchanitteash.
Let him be kept,
wadchanaj.
}

plur. {
Let us be kept,
Wadchanitteatuh.
Be ye kept,
wadchanitteak.
Let them be kept,
wadchanaj.
}

Optative Mode.

Present tense.

sing. {
I wish I be kept,
Noowaadchanittean-toh.
I wish thou be kept,
koowaadchanittean-toh.
I wish he be kept,
waadchanon-toh.
}

Present tense.

plur. {
I wish we be kept,
Noowaadchanitteanan-toh.
I wish ye be kept,
koowaadchanitteaneau-toh.
I wish they be kept,
waadchanoneau-toh.
}

Præter tense.

sing. {
I wish I was kept,
Noowaadchanitteanaz-toh.
I wish thou wast kept,
koowaadchanitteanaz-toh.
I wish he was kept,
waadchanònaz-toh.
}

Præter tense.

plur. {
I wish we were kept,
Noowaadchanitteananònuz-toh.
I wish ye were kept,
koowaadchanitteanaouz-toh.
I wish they were kept,
waadchanonaouz-toh.
}

Suppositive Mode.

Present tense.

sing.
{
When I am kept,
Wadchanitteaon.
When thou art kept,
wadchanitteaan.
When he is kept,
wadchanit noh.
}

Present tense.

plur.
{
When we are kept,
Wadchanitteaog.
When ye are kept,
wadchanitteaóg.
When they are kept,
wadchanit nag.
}

The *Præter tense* is formed by *adding* [us *or* ás] unto the *Present tense.*

Indefinite Mode.

Wadchanittéinát, *To be kept.*

✣✣N✣✤✤✤✤✤✤✤✤✤✤✤✤✤✤✤✤✤✤✤✤✤✤✤✤✤✤✤✤✤✤✤✤✤✤✤

The form *Negative* of the Verb *Substantive Passive.*

Indicative Mode.

Present tense.

sing.
{
I am not kept,
Noowadchanitteòh.
Thou art not kept,
koowadchanitteòh.
He is not kept,
Mat wadchanau.
}

Present tense.

plur.
{
We are not kept,
Noowadchanitteoumun.
Ye are not kept,
koowadchanitteoumwoo.
They are not kept,
Mat wadchanoog.
}

Præter tense.

sing.
{
I was not kept,
Noowadchanitteohp.
Thou wast not kept,
koowadchanitteohp.
He was not kept,
Mat wadchanôuop.
}

Præter tense.

plur.
{
We were not kept,
noowadchanitteoumunnonup.
Ye were not kept,
koowadchanitteoumwop
They were not kept,
Mat wadchanoop.
}

Imperative

Suppositive Mode.

Present tense.   *Present tense.*

sing. {
When I am kept,
Wadchanitteaon.
When thou art kept,
wadchanitteaan.
When he is kept,
wadchanit noh.
}

plur. {
When we are kept,
Wadchanitteaog.
When ye are kept,
wadchanitteaóg.
When they are kept,
wadchanit nag.
}

The *Præter tense* is formed by *adding* [us *or* ás] unto the
Present tense.

Indefinite Mode.

Wadchanittéinát,   *To be kept.*

✦✦*N*✦✦✦✦✦✦✦✦✦✦✦✦✦✦✦✦✦✦✦✦✦✦✦✦✦

The form *Negative* of the Verb *Substantive Passive.*

Indicative Mode.

Present tense.   *Present tense.*

sing. {
I am not kept,
Noowadchanitteòh.
Thou art not kept,
koowadchanitteòh
He is not kept,
Mat wadchanau.
}

plur. {
We are not kept,
Noowadchanitteoumun.
Ye are not kept,
koowadchanitteoumwoo.
They are not kept,
Mat wadchanoog.
}

Præter tense.   *Præter tense.*

sing. {
I was not kept,
Noowadchanitteohp.
Thou wast not kept,
koowadchanitteohp.
He was not kept,
Mat wadchanôuop.
}

plur. {
We were not kept,
noowadchanitteoumunnonup.
Ye were not kept,
koowadchanitteoumwop.
They were not kept,
Mat wadchanoop.
}

Imperative Mode of the form *Negative Passive.*

sing. {
Be thou not kept,
Wadchanittuhkon.
Let not him be kept,
wadchittekitch.
}

plur. {
Be not ye kept,
Wadchanittuhkook.
Let not them be kept,
wadchanittekhettich.
}

Suppositive Mode Passive Negative.

Present tense.

sing. {
When I am not kept,
Wadchaneumuk.
When thou art not kept,
wadchaninoomuk.
When he is not kept,
wadchanómuk.
}

Present tense.

{
The *Plural* it formed by adding (Mat) unto the form *Affirmative.*
}

The *Prater tense* is formed by *adding* [us *or* ás] to the *Present tense.*

The *Indefinite Mode Passive* Negative.

Wadchanóunát, *Not to be kept.*

I 2   A Table

63 *The* Indian *Grammar begun.*

Imperative Mode of the form *Negative Passive.*

sing. {
Be thou not kept,
Wadchanittuhkon.
Let not him be kept,
wadchittekitch.

plur. {
Be not ye kept,
Wadchanittuhkook.
Let not them be kept,
wadchanittekhettich.

Suppositive Mode Passive Negative.

Present tense.

sing. {
When I am not kept,
Wadchaneumuk.
When thou art not kept,
wadchaninoomuk.
When he is not kept,
wadchanómuk.

Present tense.

{
The *Plural* is formed by
adding (Mat) unto the
form *Affirmative.*

The *Præter tense* is formed by *adding* [us *or* ás] to the *Present tense.*

The *Indefinite Mode Passive* Negative.

Wadchanóunát,   *Not to be kept.*

A T A B L E of the Grammar of the *Suffix Verbs Af-*
Addition after the word, are fet down : As for the *Affix* or
Optative Modes ; The *Imperative* and *Suppofitive Modes* lay it
and [*Thou   him*] in the *Indicative Mode,* is the *Radicall*
Mode, is the *Radical word* without any *Affix* or *Suffix* : and

Indicative Mode.   Imperative Mode.

Prefent tenfe.   *Prater tenfe.*

1 { 1 oufh / 2 radic. / 3 unumwoo. / 4 oog }
1 { 1 unup / 2 óp / 3 unumwop / 4 opanneg }
1 { 1 unutti / 2 onti / 3 unonkquich / 4 onti }

2 { 1 eh *or* ah / 2 radic. / 3 imun / 4 oog }
2 { 1 ip / 2 op / 3 imunónup. / 4 opanneg }
2 { 1 eh / 2 radic. / 3 innean / 4 radic. }

3. { 1 uk / 2 uk / 3 oh *or* uh / 4 ukqun / 5 ukkou / 6 oh *or* uh }
3 { 1 ukup / 2 ukup / 3 opch / 4 ukqunónup / 5 ukoowop / 6 opoh }
3 { 1 itch / 2 ukqufh / 3 onch / 4 ukqutteuh / 5 ukook / 6 onch }

1 { 1 unumun / 2 óun / 3 unvinun / 4 óunónog }
1 { 1 unumunónup / 2 óunónup / 3 unumunónup / 4 óunónuppanneg }
1 { 1 unuttuh / 2 ontuh / 3 unuttuh / 4 ontuh }

2 { 1 imwoo / 2 au / 3 imun / 4 auoog }
2 { 1 imwop / 2 auop / 3 imunónup / 4 auopanneg. }
2 { 1 egk *or* ig / 2 ók / 3 inuean / 4 ók }

3 { 1 ukquog / 2 ukquog / 3 ouh / 4 ukqunonog / 5 ukoooog / 6 ouh }
3 { 1 ukuppanneg / 2 ukuppanneg / 3 auopuh / 4 ukqunónuppanneg / 5 ukooópanneg / 6 auopoh }
3 { 1 ukquttei, *or* éhettich / 2 ukqufh / 3 ahettich / 4 ukqutteuh / 5 ukook / 6 ahettich }

firmative, wherein onely the *Suffixes,* viz. The Grammatical *Prefix* , you may obferve it is ufed onely in the *Indicative* and by, and are varied onely by the *Suffix.* Alfo note, that [*I   him*] *word* with the *Affix* ; and [*Do thou   him*] in the *Imperative* what is prefixed or fuffixed to the *Radix,* is *Grammar.*

Optative Mode.

Suppofitive Mode.

Prefent tenfe.   *Præter tenfe.*   *Prefent tenfe.*   *Præter tenfe.*

1 $\left\{\begin{array}{l}\text{1 unon}\\\text{2 on}\\\text{3 uneau}\\\text{4 óneau}\end{array}\right.$ 1 $\left\{\begin{array}{l}\text{1 ununaz}\\\text{2 ónaz}\\\text{3 ununnaóuz}\\\text{4 ónaóuz}\end{array}\right.$ 1 $\left\{\begin{array}{l}\text{1 unon}\\\text{2 og}\\\text{3 unòg}\\\text{4 og}\end{array}\right.$ 1 $\left\{\begin{array}{l}\text{1 unos}\\\text{2 ogkus}\\\text{3 unógkus}\\\text{4 ogkus}\end{array}\right.$

2 $\left\{\begin{array}{l}\text{1 in}\\\text{2 on}\\\text{3 unean}\\\text{4 óneau}\end{array}\right.$ 2 $\left\{\begin{array}{l}\text{1 ineaz}\\\text{2 onaz}\\\text{3 uneanónuz}\\\text{4 ónaóuz}\end{array}\right.$ 2 $\left\{\begin{array}{l}\text{1 ean}\\\text{2 adt or at}\\\text{3 eog}\\\text{4 adt or at}\end{array}\right.$ 2 $\left\{\begin{array}{l}\text{1 eas}\\\text{2 as}\\\text{3 egkus}\\\text{4 ás}\end{array}\right.$

3 $\left\{\begin{array}{l}\text{1 ukqun}\\\text{2 ukqun}\\\text{3 on}\\\text{4 ukqunán}\\\text{5 ukquneau}\\\text{6 on}\end{array}\right.$ 3 $\left\{\begin{array}{l}\text{1 ukqunaz}\\\text{2 ukqunaz}\\\text{3 óaaz}\\\text{4 ukqunanónuz}\\\text{5 ukqunaóuz}\\\text{6 onaouz}\end{array}\right.$ 3 $\left\{\begin{array}{l}\text{1 it}\\\text{2 ukquean}\\\text{3 ont}\\\text{4 ukqueog}\\\text{5 ukqueóg}\\\text{6 ont}\end{array}\right.$ 3 $\left\{\begin{array}{l}\text{1 is}\\\text{2 ukqueas}\\\text{3 os}\\\text{4 ukqueogkus}\\\text{5 ukqueógkus}\\\text{6 os}\end{array}\right.$

1 $\left\{\begin{array}{l}\text{1 unan}\\\text{2 ónán}\\\text{3 unán}\\\text{4 ónán}\end{array}\right.$ 1 $\left\{\begin{array}{l}\text{1 unanónuz}\\\text{2 ónanónuz}\\\text{3 unanónuz}\\\text{4 ónanonuz}\end{array}\right.$ 1 $\left\{\begin{array}{l}\text{1 unog}\\\text{2 ogkut}\\\text{3 unog}\\\text{4 ogku}\end{array}\right.$ 1 $\left\{\begin{array}{l}\text{1 unogkus}\\\text{2 ogkutus}\\\text{3 unogkus}\\\text{4 ogkutus}\end{array}\right.$

2 $\left\{\begin{array}{l}\text{1 unean}\\\text{2 oneau}\\\text{3 unean}\\\text{4 óneau}\end{array}\right.$ 2 $\left\{\begin{array}{l}\text{1 ineaóuz}\\\text{2 ónaóuz}\\\text{3 ineanonuz}\\\text{4 ónaouz}\end{array}\right.$ 2 $\left\{\begin{array}{l}\text{1 eóg}\\\text{2 óg}\\\text{3 eóg}\\\text{4 òg}\end{array}\right.$ 2 $\left\{\begin{array}{l}\text{1 eógkus}\\\text{2 ògkus}\\\text{3 eógkus}\\\text{4 ógkus}\end{array}\right.$

3 $\left\{\begin{array}{l}\text{1 ukquneau}\\\text{2 ukqunean}\\\text{3 óneau}\\\text{4 ukqunán}\\\text{5 ukquneau}\\\text{6 oneau}\end{array}\right.$ 3 $\left\{\begin{array}{l}\text{1 ukqunaouz}\\\text{2 ukqunaouz}\\\text{3 ónaouz}\\\text{4 ukqunanonuz}\\\text{5 ukqunaóuz}\\\text{6 ónaóuz}\end{array}\right.$ 3 $\left\{\begin{array}{l}\text{1 hettit}\\\text{2 ukquean}\\\text{3 áhettit}\\\text{4 ukqueog}\\\text{5 ukqueóg}\\\text{6 ahettit}\end{array}\right.$ 3 $\left\{\begin{array}{l}\text{1 ehettis}\\\text{2 ukqueas}\\\text{3 ahettis}\\\text{4 ukqueogkus}\\\text{5 ukqueógkus}\\\text{6 ahettis.}\end{array}\right.$

Onely remember that [toh] *is to be annexed note every perfon and variation in this Mode.*

The Indian *Grammar begun.*

A TABLE of the Grammar of the *Suffix Verbs Af-*
Addition after the word, are set down : As for the Affix or
Optative Modes, The *Imperative* and *Suppositive Modes* lay it
and [*Thou   him*] in the *Indicative Mode,* is the *Radicall*
Mode, is the *Radical word* without any *Affix* or *Suffix* : and

<table>
<tr><td colspan="4" align="center">Indicative Mode.</td><td align="center">Imperative Mode</td></tr>
<tr><td colspan="2">*Present tense.*</td><td colspan="2">*Præter tense*</td><td></td></tr>
</table>

		Present		Præter		Imperative
1	1	oush	1	unup	1	unutti
	2	radic.	2	óp	2	onti
	3	unumwoo	3	unumwop	3	unokquich
	4	oog	4	opanneg	4	onti
2	1	eh *or* ah	1	ip	1	eh
	2	radic.	2	op	2	radic.
	3	imun	3	imunónup	3	innean
	4	oog	4	opanneg	4	radic.
3	1	uk	1	ukup	1	itch
	2	uk	2	ukup	2	ukqush
	3	oh *or* uh	3	opch	3	onch
	4	ukqun	4	ukqunónup	4	ukqutteuh
	5	ukkou	5	ukoowop	5	ukook
	6	oh or uh	6	opoh	6	onch
1	1	unumun	1	unumunónup	1	unuttuh
	2	óun	2	óunónup	2	ontuh
	3	unuinun	3	unumunónup	3	unuttuh
	4	óunónog	4	óunónuppanneg	4	ontuh
2	1	imwoo	1	imwop	1	egk *or* ig
	2	au	2	auop	2	ók
	3	imun	3	imunónup	3	inuean
	4	auoog	4	auopanneg	4	ók
3	1	ukquog	1	ukuppanneg	1	ukquttei, *or* éhettich
	2	ukquog	2	ukuppanneg	2	ukqush
	3	ouh	3	auopuh	3	ahettich
	4	ukquonog	4	ukqunónuppanneg	4	ukqutteuh
	5	ukoooog	5	ukooópanneg	5	ukook
	6	ouh	6	auopoh	6	ahettich

65 *The* Indian *Grammar begun.*

firmative, wherein onely the *Suffixes*, viz. The Grammatical *Prefix*, you may observe it is used onely in the *Indicative* and by, and are varied onely by the *Suffix*. Also note, that [*I him*] *word* with the *Affix* ; and [*Do thou him*] in the *Imperative* what is prefixed or suffixed to the *Radix*, is *Grammar*.

	Optative Mode.		Suppositive Mode	
	Present tense.	*Præter tense.*	*Present tense*	*Præter tense*
I 1	unon	ununaz	unon	unos
2	on	ónaz	og	ogkus
3	uneau	ununnaóuz	unog	unógkus
4	óneau	ónaóuz	og	ogkus
2 1	in	ineaz	ean	eas
2	on	onaz	adt *or* at	as
3	unean	uneanónuz	eog	egkus
4	óneau	óuaóuz	adt *or* at	ás
3 1	ukqun	ukqunaz	it	is
2	ukqun	ukqunaz	ukquean	ukqueas
3	on	óaaz	ont	os
4	ukqunán	ukqunanónuz	ukqueog	ukqueogkus
5	ukquneau	ukqunaóuz	ukqueóg	ukqueógkus
6	on	onaouz	ont	os
I 1	unan	unanónuz	unog	unogkus
2	ónán	ónanónuz	ogkut	ogkutus
3	unán	unanónuz	unog	unogkus
4	ónán	ónanonuz	ogku	ogkutus
2 1	unean	ineaóuz	eóg	eógkus
2	oneau	ónaóuz	óg	ògkus
3	unean	ineanonuz	eóg	eógkus
4	óneau	ónaouz	òg	ógkus
3 1	ukquneau	ukqunaouz	hettit	ehettis
2	ukqunean	ukqunaouz	ukquean	ukqueas
3	óneau	ónaouz	áhettit	ahettis
4	ukqunán	ukqunanonuz	ukqueog	ukqueogkus
5	ukquneau	ukqunaóuz	ukqueóg	ukqueógkus
6	oneau	óuaóuz	ahettit	ahettis

onely remember that [toh] is to be annexed unto every person and variation in this Mode.

I Have now *finished what I shall do at present : And in a word or two to satisfie the prudent Enquirer how I found-out these new wayes of* Grammar, *which no other Learned Language (so farre as I know) useth ; I thus inform him :* God first put into my heart a compassion over their poor Souls, and a desire to teach them to know Christ, and to bring them into his Kingdome. *Then presently I found out (by Gods wise providence)* a pregnant witted young man, who had been a Servant in an English house, who pretty well understood our Language, better then he could speak it, and well understood his own Language, and hath a clear pronunciation : *Him I made my* Interpreter. *By his help I translated the* Commandments, *the* Lords Prayer, *and many* Texts of Scripture : also I compiled both Exhortations and Prayers by his help. *I diligently marked the* difference of their Grammar from ours : when I found the way of them, I would pursue a Word, a Noun, a Verb, through all variations I could think of. And thus I came at it. We must not sit still, and look for Miracles : Up, and be doing, and the Lord will be with thee. Prayer and Pains, through Faith in Christ Jesus, will do any thing. Nil tam deficile quod non —— I do believe and hope, that the Gospel shall be spread to all the Ends of the Earth, and dark Corners of the World, by such a way, and by such Instruments as the Churches shall send forth for that end and purpose. Lord hasten those good dayes, and pour out that good Spirit upon thy people. Amen

F I N I S.

I Have now finished what I shall do at present : And in a word or two to satisfie the prudent Enquirer how I found-out these new wayes of Grammar, which no other Learned Language (so farre as I know) useth ; I thus inform him : God first put into my heart a compassion over their poor Souls, and a desire to teach them to know Christ, and to bring them into his Kingdome. Then presently I found out (by Gods wise providence) a pregnant witted young man, who had been a Servant in an English house, who pretty well understood our Language, better then he could speak it, and well understood his own Language, and hath a clear pronunciation : Him I made my Interpreter. By his help I translated the Commandments, the Lords Prayer, and many Texts of Scripture : also I compiled both Exhortations and Prayers by his help. I diligently marked the difference of their Grammar from ours : when I found the way of them, I would pursue a Word, a Noun, a Verb, through all variations I could think of. And thus I came at it. We must not sit still, and look for Miracles : Up, and be doing, and the Lord will be with thee. Prayer and Pains through Faith in Christ Jesus, will do anything. Nil tam deficile quod non— I do believe and hope, that the Gospel shall be spread to all the Ends of the Earth, and dark Corners of the World, by such a way, and by such Instruments as the Churches shall send forth for that end and purpose. Lord hasten those good dayes, and pour out that good Spirit upon thy people. Amen.

F I N I S.

Colophon

This edition of
The Indian Grammar Begun: or,
An Essay to bring the Indian Language into Rules,
was originally printed by Marmaduke Johnson in 1666
at Cambridge, Massachusetts.
It was set in the then very popular Caslon with the addition
of a special character
"∞",
requested by John Eliot.
"Especially we have more frequent use of [o *and* ∞]
then other Languages have: and our [∞] doth
always sound as it doth in these
English words (*moody, book.*)"
This character was created anew by Roger Gordy
specifically for this edition,
to be used in conjunction with Adobe's Caslon.
The two ornamental borders used in the original
have been recreated by Mr. Gordy
by scanning the originals,
bringing them into Adobe Photoshop,
and digitally cleaning by hand. Those digital
images were then exported to Adobe Illustrator
to create these clean, modern versions.

Foreword © 2001 by Caring Hands
The digitally modified original and the modified modern typesetting of
The Indian Grammar Begun: or, An Essay to bring the Indian Language into Rules, for the Help of such
as desire to Learn the same, for the furtherance of the Gospel among them,
the two modern digitized borders and the character "∞" © 2001 by Roger Gordy